Walking Coast to Coast

An unfit person's guide

Also by the same author:
The Hyphen In-Between:
An Autobiography of an Ordinary Man
Paperback – Amazon Publishing 16 Feb. 2023

Initially conceived as 'something to leave behind for his descendants to read one day', this book is the author's life journey from his birth to his 60th birthday. An autobiographical perception of global events is interspersed with personal memories, from playing in coal-blackened snow as a child, watching England win the World Cup, man landing on the moon, to living through times inhabited by hippies, greasers, skinheads, Hell's Angels, and football hooligans. Eating tv dinners while watching the television programs of the different eras, surviving 'Winters of Discontent', the 'Thatcher years', Royal weddings, Royal divorces, and terrorism.
The author's adventures and misadventures are both funny and sad; sometimes painful and sometimes thought-provoking. A journey through time, which will undoubtedly jog the reader's memories.
'Everyone has a story to tell – this is mine.'
Chris Vaughan

Print length - 800 pages
Language - English

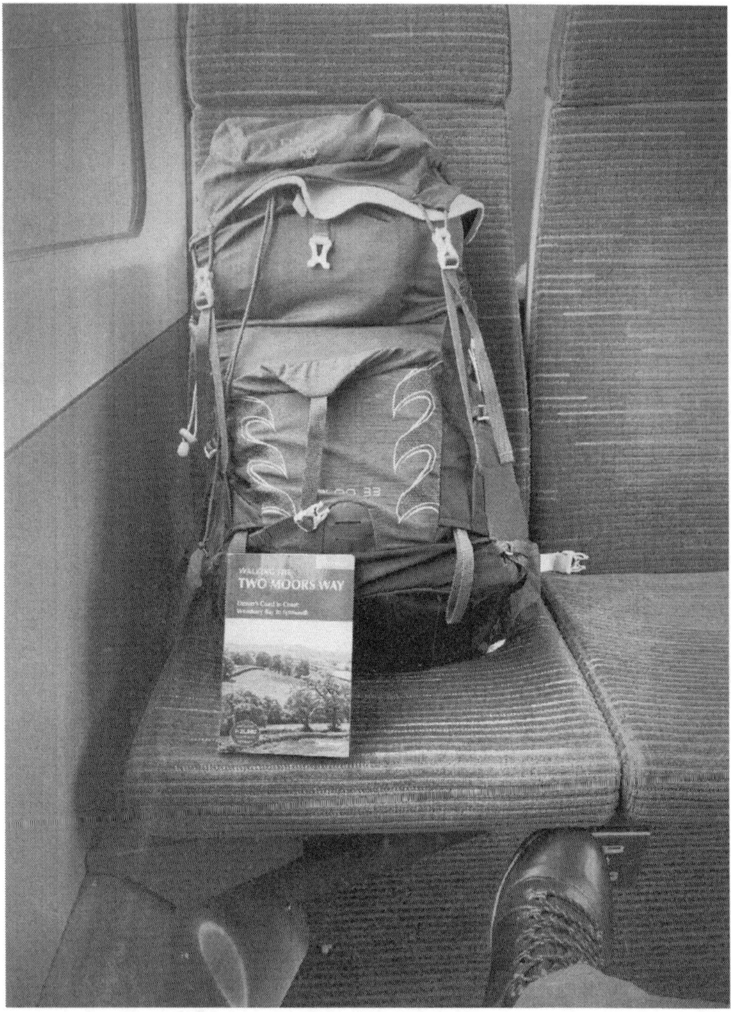
TWO MOORS WAY

For Lee

Preface

When middle-age has come and gone, and retirement beckons from over the not too far horizon, one is faced with choices.

Option one: You can either retire to the sofa, eat snacks, watch Countdown, and start to put on weight where you begin to resemble a beached mammal. At some point shortly thereafter, Greenpeace will be alerted. You will start to take a keen interest in television advertisements portraying the latest fashion in mobility scooters, your wife will disappear and shack up with a fitness instructor in the South of France and leave you with the dog.

Option two: You can become almost fanatical about trying to keep fit, join a gym, go on strenuous walks, dye your hair, and buy a classic sports car. You start to play squash and tennis, then suffer a fatal heart attack. Life can be so unfair.

Option three: You can opt for the middle road. Retain your poor diet of cheeseburgers and a few pints, followed by a cigarette or two. Feeling remorseful a day or so later, you go on a walk for a while, in the belief that it will offset the shortcomings of your lifestyle. Your wife stays with you but asks you for the umpteenth time to quit smoking. You secretly watch Countdown when she's not looking.

I chose option three.

Just opposite the Exmoor Centre in Lynmouth is a metal statue called 'The Walker'. It was created by a local lad called Richard Graham, a metal fabricator, who goes by the nickname of 'Goggs'. I'd seen the statue many times but wasn't really aware of its significance until relatively recently. It heralds a position where three walks converge: the South-West Coast Path, the Coleridge Way, and the Two Moors Way. As my choice of option suggests, I do a little bit of walking: it is a good way to keep fit I suppose. But I'm not really a 'walker' – I'm slightly overweight, more than slightly over 60, and I smoke. I surprised myself with an answer which I gave to my local GP who asked me how long I had smoked. 'Over half a century.' There's a thought.

I can't recall when the idea of walking across Devon materialised. It probably popped into my head while I was out walking one of my normal routes, over the top of a hill which towers opposite the Valley of Rocks, very close to where I live in Lynton. I was more than likely having a seated rest from my exertions walking up to the top, where the views are fairly impressive, to say the least. Since I've lived here, friends and family have come to visit, and invariably, during their stay, we go on a walk somewhere – nothing too strenuous, just an amble around, usually ending up in a pub or a cafe.

During a telephone conversation with my son Lee, we discussed the possibility of undertaking a long walk together. Numerous conversations followed during January 2023, where we started to formulate our plan. My state retirement was forthcoming in late May – wouldn't it be great to undertake a nice long walk and finish up having a party at the end of it? We both decided it would be. We would undertake the walk the week before my 66th birthday and celebrate this auspicious day, my retirement, and of course, our physical effort. For the party, once again I would utilise the local Cottage Inn, and a local band called 'Basil's Blues Band' (who I had also used for my 60th birthday party), and invite the whole village, as well as close friends and family. I made a slight amendment to the timetable: I didn't want to finish the walk on party day, heroically staggering into the festivities sweating like a racehorse, and acknowledging the congratulations of all present with a limp wave, before collapsing dramatically onto the floor. A revival exercise would follow, by pouring beer between my weak, quivering lips. Instead, I suggested we finished the walk the day before, which would give both Lee and myself time to rest up, prior to the Devon party onslaught.

The finer points of our endeavour were further discussed. How were we going to undertake the walk? Almost immediately, we both dismissed the idea of camping. Nowadays, tents which weigh as much as a butterfly's sex organs, weren't the problem. The problem was all of the other stuff: clothes, a sleeping bag, cooking stuff, food, water. All that lot would weigh as much as an elephant's sex organs. I like my comforts, and so does Lee. So it was decided that we would stay in some sort of accommodation each night during our walk: the responsibility of making our overnight arrangements would be made by both of us, on an alternate basis. Additionally, I decided that I didn't need to cover every square inch of the Two Moors Way. All I wanted to do, was to just walk across Devon somehow. On parts of our walk, we would encounter and walk along some of the official route, but for the time being, I was going to be quite happy with a simple traverse across Devon, using quiet, country lanes, bits of moorland, and footpaths through woodlands.

The logistics were sorted, and Saturday 27th May 2023 was set as the party date: For our walk, we would both make our separate ways to Plymouth on Friday 19th May and meet up there. In the interim, Lee and I, literally, stepped up our walks. I pounded and sweated around the local hills, averaging around 2.5 miles per hour. This doesn't sound like a lot (for some who are fitter, it isn't), but you need to appreciate some of the hills 'around these 'ere parts'. As

I put a reasonable amount of effort into my trudgery, an enormous wet patch would materialise on the front and back of my tee shirt, and I would emit a sweaty bouquet. Embarrassingly, just as my exudations were at their maximum, I would pass other people who were out for a ramble, silently apologising to them for my appearance and odour, while they looked and smelt as fresh as newly washed linen. To try to avoid other people, sometimes I would catch the 'Exmoor Coaster' bus service, alight at County Gate, and walk the five miles or so back to Lynmouth. During the uphill parts of these walks, I discovered that I wasn't seeing very much in the way of scenic views, unless I actually stopped. My eyes were firmly focused on my boots as I was trying to maintain a reasonable pace. I started to become a bit bored – the walks I was undertaking were much more like exercise, rather than any envisaged pleasant stroll.

As time went by and May arrived, I started to become slightly impatient. I felt physically ok and couldn't wait to go. I believed that I would be fine walking coast to coast: it would a nice adventure, and even nicer to undertake it with an offspring. And, as Lee had pointed out, even if our pace was only two miles an hour, we would still cover a respectable distance if we walked for eight or nine hours.

My relatively new backpack was crammed with clothing – nothing too heavy, as the weather forecast for the week indicated that it was going to be sunny and warm. But I packed my thin, waterproof jacket and trousers just in case.

I went to bed early the night before the off, and dreamt of myself striding purposefully through moorland, fording small streams, and breezing up woodland footpaths, cruising past other stumbling hikers with ease. I awoke early. Maybe one of the stumbling hikers in my dream was me.

The Day Before: Friday 19th

My better half, Kirsty, presented me with a gift. Unbeknown to me, she had purchased a large box of individually wrapped, chocolate-covered flapjacks, taken thirty of them, and placed them beside my backpack. 'It'll keep your energy up,' she said. I needed a fair amount of my energy just to pick one up, they were that heavy. And somehow, I had to squeeze them into the already overflowing backpack. When I had finally managed that, I picked it up and found that it weighed five times as much as it had previously. In addition, the straps of the pack now made a strange, stretching noise: it sounded like they were complaining.

Just before half-past two in the afternoon I boarded the 310 Filers bus service to Barnstaple train station. The journey took about an hour, so I had ten minutes to spare before the 15.35 train to Exeter St. Davids departed. The train journey (Tarka Line) is always a pleasant one and is a bit twee: the majority being a single line track, and a bellpush inside the train if you want to alight at a 'request stop'. Someone waiting at such a station must stick their arm out to hail the train driver. Momentarily, it felt like I was back in my youth on a London bus – minus the rubbish and the weirdos. It either passed through or stopped at stations I was likely to walk past on my walk back. A momentary thought of defeatism crept through my mind – if the walk was that bad well, I could just catch a train home. Enough. The train pulled into Exter St. Davids, and I had eight minutes to scurry over a bridge to Platform 4 for the Exeter to Plymouth train. At this point, Lee, having travelled over from Essex, had already passed through Exeter and was ahead of me by about twenty minutes. His journey had been slightly problematic however: an 'incident' on the line between Paddington and Exeter had necessitated a detour via Bristol – usually the train would journey through Reading.

Lee was waiting for me at Plymouth Station, adorned with his backpack. He waved a small video camera at me as I progressed towards him – so, we were to undertake some filming of our exploits. Well, Lee was at any rate. My time, apparently, in front of the camera, would be spent verbally rambling about our physical rambling.

Chatting as we went, we walked about a mile or so to a Premier Inn at Lockyers Quay, where I had reserved a twin room for the night. On our arrival, we were advised to book dinner at an adjoining restaurant, as it was invariably busy on a Friday night, so we took the receptionist's advice and reserved a table for eight o'clock. After dumping our gear into our room, we made our way across a large carpark to a pub which, apart from the staff, we were the only two humans in the place. It had been good salesmanship on behalf of the receptionist. By the time we had finished our meal of a burger, (the size of a baby's head), chips, and a couple of ales each, a nominal six other people had sat down to dine. Lee telephoned a local taxi company and arranged for us to be collected the following morning at seven-thirty.

We made our way back to our room which was stiflingly hot. Lee was averse to opening the window as were on the ground floor, so I endured a fitful sleep until four in the morning, when I found myself fully awake and totally dehydrated. I felt like I had been asleep in a kiln. I drank my way through a large amount of water, sank back onto my bed, and dozed on and off until around half past six. After a quick shower, I pulled on my 'camo' trousers, a tee shirt and my heavy boots, poured myself a coffee and went outside for a smoke. I was ready to go.

Devon Coast To Coast Walk
Two Moors Way
Erme Court / Watermark
Devon Coast To Coast Walk
Erme Plym Trail
Town Centre
Glanvilles Mill
Youth/ Leisure Centre

Saturday 20th

Our taxi arrived at approximately half-seven and was driven by Lisa, a pleasant, peroxide-headed, late forty-year-old. Her nature was such that she agreed to our request to go to Wembury Bay via a McDonalds drive-through on the outskirts of Plymouth for a breakfast. Our reasoning for such a dining experience was that, well, basically both Lee and I like them. And I have a bodily girth to maintain. We arrived at Wembury at around eight, having spent the journey being teased nasally by the scent emanating from the take-away bag that Lee was carrying on his lap in the rear seat. I engaged Lisa in a varied conversation about her vocation in life and how she had eventually ended up undertaking the job she was currently doing. Including her previous husbands and partners, she began to reveal her rather convoluted life-story, which had more twists than a 1960's dance hall. I was somewhat pleased when Wembury hove into view – at that point we had only covered the first couple of decades or so of her life story and, intrigued as I was, there just wasn't enough time for her to bring me fully up to date. We each have a limited lifespan, after all. Lee and I bade Lisa farewell, turned our gaze seaward and commenced with our breakfasts, as Lisa disappeared back in the direction of Plymouth.

I munched through my hash brown as Lee disappeared past the closed café (previously a 12th century mill) onto the beach to gather two stones – one for him and one for me. He returned with two small white pebbles – our symbolic start stones, with the idea that two more would be collected from Lynmouth beach once the journey had been completed. I stared at the Great Mewstone in the bay, a large triangular lump of rock, which is about a mile offshore and was acquired by The National Trust in 2006, who promptly turned it into a nature reserve and barred any visitors. Apart from themselves of course. Prior to this however, in 1744, a local individual named Samuel Wakeman was found guilty of a minor crime and initially was due to be transported to Australia for seven years. A clemency plea was upheld however, and he ended up serving his sentence living on the Mewstone instead. He must have employed the services of a fairly astute lawyer; somehow his wife was allowed to accompany him in his exile - they even raised a family there. They remained on the Mewstone when the sentence was completed, by masquerading as a warden against poachers, and paying his rent by supplying rabbits for the Manor House table. In reality, he undertook a little bit of smuggling himself, (who'd have thought?) was eventually caught and evicted. The only other visitor of note to this remote rock was the painter J. M. W.

Turner – he hopped on and off the rock a couple of times, and his paintings of the Mewstone are retained in the Tate Gallery in London and the National Gallery of Ireland in Dublin.

Muffins chomped, hash browns swallowed, and coffees slung down hatches, we started off towards the village of Wembury up the small lane and past the Marine Centre (which was shut). Had we been rigorously following the coast-to-coast trail, at the top of the lane where it met Church Road, we should have crossed over and headed down a bridleway in the direction of a place called Higher Ford Farm. Instead, we followed Church Road into Wembury – just about all of it uphill. We didn't know it then, but a pattern of starting each day with an uphill slog was to become the norm. We declined getting a new hairstyle at a local emporium called Blush, nor, having omitted to bring any dogs with us, did we venture into Natalie's Dog Grooming Salon. Instead, we continued onto Knighton Road, passing The Odd Wheel (bistro cum pub cum wine bar) and wheezed to a halt like a couple of steam shunters in a siding, outside the Wembury Convenience Store. Enhancing its convenience status was a wooden bench provided outside which I slumped onto, while Lee went inside to purchase some bottles of water.

With a bit of subsequent research, it transpired that Wembury has, over time, produced evidence of worked flint dated to around 10,000 years ago. Less chronologically distant, roman coins have also been found and, even less distant, about 1000 years ago, a Saxon church dedicated to Saint Werburgh was built. Werburgh was a princess born in Staffordshire, and the daughter of a certain King Wulfhere of Mercia and his wife Ermenilda. Werburgh had a couple of tricks up her sleeve: she apparently restored a dead goose to life (the badge of a gaggle of geese was adopted as proof of this) and, eight years after her death in AD 700 during a re-siting of her remains, it was discovered that her body was completely intact - a sign of divine favour apparently. Currently, she is the patron saint of Chester and, in case you're feeling hungry, her feast day is February 3rd.

Water acquired, Lee sat next to me on the bench, and we squinted at our maps and booklets in the bright sunshine and planned our next move. By visiting the shop, we had overshot the hiker's route from Wembury to Ivybridge – commonly called the 'Erme-Plym Trail' - but by backtracking a few yards and heading up Traine Road for roughly half a mile, we rejoined the trail at Hollacombe. We walked along a pavement by the side of a road for a couple of minutes before we turned right onto a footpath through a wood. A few steps in and there was a table on our right with a note telling us to 'help ourselves' to free drinking water which I thought was a nice gesture, but as Lee and I were both weighed down with the stuff we had recently purchased from the Wembury Convenience Store, we passed the free offering and continued to walk downhill through the woods. At the bottom we crossed a stile: 'dog-friendly' as my Cicerone guide indicated. A 'dog-friendly stile' was just one variation of a means of crossing a boundary, whether it was field to field, or an entrance (or exit) from a roadway to a field; before the walk I hadn't realised there were so many different styles of stiles (as it were), merely considering them as another obstacle to delay me getting to a hostelry somewhere where I could have a nice meal with a beer. But, during our venture, we were to hop over or walk through standard stiles, alternative stiles, stiles over wire, stone wall stiles, bridle gates, kissing gates and step through gates. This particular dog friendly stile was an entrance to a large earth field. I am aware that technically, all fields are made of earth, but invariably they do have crops or grasses covering them. This one was dry, grey-brown mud. As we crossed the field below a largish dwelling called Spriddlestone House, our boots kicked up clouds of dust which ascended briefly, before comfortably settling back onto various parts of our clothing, giving us the appearance of cement factory workers coming off shift.

The field of mud transitioned into a grassy lane with a gate at the end where we emerged into the small hamlet of Spriddlestone itself. Like squaddies on a parade ground, we undertook a smart right then left, climbed a few steps carved into a field edge, and passed through a kissing gate. Another field, another gate, another field, another gate, followed by a climb and then a descent through a woodland down to Cofflete Creek. There is a small bridge across the creek (once owned by the Great Western Railway) and one we had seen many times on various videos concerning the Two Moors Way. We sat for a few minutes patting off dust – a drink, a smoke for me, another drink of water and we were on our way again.

Although it was around mid-morning, the temperature was beginning to rise, and it was pleasant to find that our next section was through a shaded lane, cut through a dark woodland which had high stonework along the sides. The reason behind this became clear when we passed through a tunnel under a bridge. Above, us, according to the guidebook, were the remnants of a railway track which used to operate between Plymouth and Yealmpton. We ascended another hill - a fairly steep one – which ended in a small flight of steps with a gate which I slumped over, gasping for breath like a goldfish on a carpet. The footpath beyond ended at a stone stile; a short distance further on we reached the A379. A right and a left led us onto a road called Lodge Lane, which we ascended in conjunction with the steadily rising temperature. We punctuated our huffing and puffing by drinking more water and, with steam beginning to emanate from our ears, we finally reached the top of the hill where, after thirty seconds of recovery panting, we subsequently descended airily down a small road called Legion Lane, arriving at a point some 300 yards further along the A379 in Brixton. This all seemed a bit pointless to me. Why not just walk along the road? It would have been far less effort. But it hadn't been as pointless as I assumed. Lee informed me that on our descent down Legion Lane he had caught sight of a girl sunbathing butt naked in a semi-concealed garden way off to our left. With sweat flowing copiously from my forehead into my eyes like a waterfall, I had failed to see anything, but Lee assured me it was true. Feeling somewhat short-changed, I followed Lee east along the main road past St. Mary's Church and the 'Speculation Gallery' - the latter I thought ironically named as it was shut, and there was no indication of its hours of business.

The next bit of the guidebook instructed us to do more 'off-roading', but we were getting wise to the book's foibles. We had just undertaken the two longest sides of a scalene triangle at a cost of three quarters of a mile to attain a three-hundred-yard progression on our journey and we weren't going to get sucked in like that again. In addition, between us, there was only a fifty percent chance of espying a sunbathing girl, naked or otherwise. In all fairness however, the distance of the next 'offroad' bit was approximately the same distance (about a mile) to walking along the road; once Lee had checked on his phone that there was a pavement all the way to Yealmpton, we both agreed it would be easier on the feet if we just walked along the side of the A379, which is what we did, arriving in Yealmpton a short time later.

As we were passing the Volunteer pub I asked a fairly ancient individual, who I presumed to be local as she was carrying two bags of shopping, where we might be able to obtain a cup of tea. She stopped, put down one of the bags and pointed across the road in a direction which indicated that we should cross the road and muttered 'Nelli's'. She stooped, reclaimed her bag – I assumed her exercise routine was now finished for the day - and wandered past us in the direction in which we had arrived. We crossed the road and in less than fifty yards arrived at Nelli's Village Café. It was fairly busy, and I had a premonition of a long wait. Lee dropped his backpack and scuttled off, leaving a trail of airborne dust particles in his wake, to an open doorway where people were queueing. I unburdened myself of my backpack, laid it to rest by the small courtyard wall, and opened one of the bottles of water, taking a long swig under the clear blue sky and bright sunshine, all the time looking for a table where some shade was offered. But there weren't any – all were taken and none of the occupants appeared to be leaving anytime soon. I sat on the wall and had a smoke while checking that my rather costly waterproof coat hadn't become loose and fallen off somewhere. I hadn't had any more room in my backpack, so had tied it on to one of the shoulder straps (it remained there for the rest of our journey, as every day was a scorcher). A thermometer on the courtyard wall indicated that currently it was 20°. Coinciding with Lee's emergence from the queue, a couple left the table closest to me, so we immediately took possession of it. I looked at Lee.

'Where's the tea?' I asked.

'They're making it,' he responded. 'They're pretty old in there,' he added as a way of explanation. I nodded sagely.

Ten minutes later, a young blond-haired girl appeared carrying assorted crockery and a teapot on a tray and placed it onto our table.

'Coo – ta' I said, as Lee immediately became 'mother' and busied himself with the teapot: I surreptitiously munched on a flapjack.

Feeling slightly refreshed, we resumed our walk along the A379 road from Yealmpton to Yealmbridge, a distance of around half a mile, crossing the Yealm river bridge just before entering the latter. Thinking that we had cut enough off of the proper route for the day, we crossed the road and headed up to a small collection of houses called Dunstone. We soon found ourselves back in fields after passing through the hamlet, and continued along the edge of one, passing a 'veteran ash tree' (as stated in the guidebook) heading for a woodland, before we realised we hadn't got things quite right. We stopped and discussed the matter, commenting on the fact that although we had never been here before, we strangely knew we had gone wrong. We backtracked a few hundred yards until we were halfway along the field, stopped again, and looked in all directions. There was a gate behind us leading to a downward sloping hill. That couldn't be right – although it was back toward the A379 of which we were walking roughly parallel. Looking to our left were the woodlands which we thought were the ones indicated in the guidebook, but we couldn't get through to them as they were fenced off. To our right was no good as that was the way we had just come from. Straight ahead of us was a rising field bordered in the distance by a thick hedge. Dammit! Which way? Then we looked a little harder. Immediately behind us near the gate was a post indicating the footpath heading off at forty-five degrees across the field to our left and towards a stile, which was only barely noticeable. Having solved the alfresco escape room task, back on track we crossed the field and over the stile and headed into another field, where the track eventually descended into a lane back onto the Erme-Plym trail. After walking through a rather picturesque woodland called Flete Wood and emerging onto a meadow, a large building called Flete House came into view. The building, dating from Saxon times, had varied uses through time – initially gentry (the Damarell family, the Hele family, the Bulteel family), then as a maternity hospital during and after the Second World War (Dave Hill of the 1970's pop group Slade was born there in 1946). It was then acquired by the Mildmay family, used as a location for a BBC television series, owned by the 'Country Houses Association' and finally went into liquidation in 2003. I personally hope the BBC goes the same way.

A 'little-used lane' (according to the guidebook), with woods on either side, guided us in a northerly direction. Halfway along the lane we decided to take a short break, indulge ourselves in some more water and dine on half a flapjack each. I dropped my backpack and sat on a fallen tree trunk with my feet extending onto the lane and rolled a smoke. Lee decided that not only did he need to take liquid on board, he also needed to drain some out of his body, so, as the lane was 'little-used', he began to avail himself of the leafy surroundings. With impeccable timing and Lee in 'mid-stream', a small white van came whistling past us. This caused Lee some angst - I merely had to withdraw my feet from the lane about six inches to ensure they weren't flattened. More vehicles came along the lane, from both directions. The 'little-used lane' was obviously utilised as a local rat-run, and Lee had to complete his wastewater management in stages. I chuckled my way through my half flapjack, amused by Lee's misfortune and uncomfortable stance.

After our allotted rest, we continued through the woods until we rejoined the A379. We crossed the River Erme at a location called Sequer's Bridge, where a footpath on the northern side of the road, running parallel to the river, would lead us past Ermington towards Ivybridge. It was at this point I began to notice, more and more, that the soles of my feet were becoming somewhat sore. Although we had believed that walking along roadways would be 'easier on the feet', it was becoming apparent that my boots, good for walks through muddy tracks and trails, weren't totally ideal for walking long distances on asphalt. Lee was wearing walking trainers, which were slightly better suited for most of our endeavour, but he was suffering from a couple of blisters, probably attributable to a lack of preparatory hill-walking through muddy woodlands, adorned with tough root structures growing across pathways. To be fair, he lived in Holland-on-Sea in Essex, an area not really noted for having a seriously rugged terrain. The backs of my calves also hurt, and I began to feel grumpy and whingy. In retrospect I now know that I didn't have the right mindset. As my friend Paul had told me a month or so earlier, 'It's a walk Chris. You should enjoy it'. Having read several books and articles since I am now wiser – the first day or so of a long walk are always the most difficult. For the moment I was content to grouch, though it made for little comfort as it was solely to myself – Lee was a hundred yards ahead and safely out of earshot.

We followed the river for some time, continuously walking along field edges, sometimes occupied by sheep, others by cattle, (as there was no one else around, I ensured I grumbled loudly at both groups of animals, which stared at me in a totally unsympathetic manner), eventually emerging onto a road called Keaton Lane, a couple of miles short of our destination. A small hamlet called Cleeve was passed through and it was this point I decided I'd had just about enough for the day. My feet were absolutely killing me – it felt like I was constantly walking on a bed of nails - so I sat on a rock next to a private gateway for about fifteen minutes, wailing like a New Orleans funeral mourner. I should have carried on another hundred yards or so, as our trek took us into the Ivybridge Football Club and there was a game on. It would have been far preferable to sit and watch the match for fifteen minutes. Oh well. We plodded past the game, and also the South Devon Tennis Centre, although I was definitely in no mood for tennis. A footpath alongside the river on our left led us under a road bridge which was conveying traffic on the main A38 Devon Expressway. As the soles of my feet burned and the backs of my calves shrieked at me, I hobbled past the Ivybridge Leisure Centre and the Ivybridge Town Hall. I joked grumpily with Lee that we should have taken the opportunity of a haircut at Blush in Wembury, as the barber's shop we now passed on our left was far more expensive. He laughed through gritted teeth as we passed a Tesco Express and found ourselves in Fore Street. We turned right, shuffled another two hundred yards and arrived at our sanctuary for the night – The Sportsmans Inn.

Lee and I had already agreed that as soon as our walking day was over (indicated by our arrival at a pub), our first drink would be a pint of ice-cold lager shandy. Lee went to the bar, and I went to the reception desk to book us into our room. Something had gone slightly askew with the booking – we had a room each – at twice the price. As I was responsible for booking this particular stop, my bank balance had to account for this error. I was too tired to argue about a room booking, so I just nodded wearily and accepted two sets of keys. It was a little after five, so I reserved a table for dinner at seven-thirty and wandered outside to the beer garden to dump the backpack, roll a cigarette, and drink an ice-cold pint. Lee dutifully appeared with two pints of our pre-determined drink which, I happily noted, had beads of condensation running down the outside of the glasses. I had similar beads of liquid running down the outside of my body. We clinked glasses and congratulated ourselves on our efforts of the day.

Three lads with hiking gear were also in the beer garden and they had just finished the same walk as us. We chatted and joked for a while; my feet and calves relishing the absence of any impact on them. A couple sat drinking and smoking at another table – he looked a bit rough and ready: she was attired in what I could only describe as a tribute rock and roll outfit. Inquiries revealed that she was the singer booked for tonight's entertainment in the pub, and he was her roadie / manager / boyfriend. I apologetically informed them that although I was sure she was wonderful at her craft, I was dog-tired to a point where I would be amazed if I didn't fall asleep head-first into my dinner, so they would have to accept the fact that I probably would not be able to make such a lively evening.

Lee and I were seated at seven-thirty, and pie and chips were the fare of the evening, along with two more beers: proper ales this time. We were in our rooms an hour later – I showered, eliminating the last remaining soil particles from my person, crawled into bed and checked my phone – it was nine o'clock and the sunlight was still streaming through the flimsy curtains. The night was young, but I wasn't. I was tired to the point where I didn't care what time it was. What I did care about were the calculations Lee and I had carried out during dinner. Today we had walked just shy of fifteen miles and it had taken us eight hours. That's less than two miles an hour – this was going to be hard.

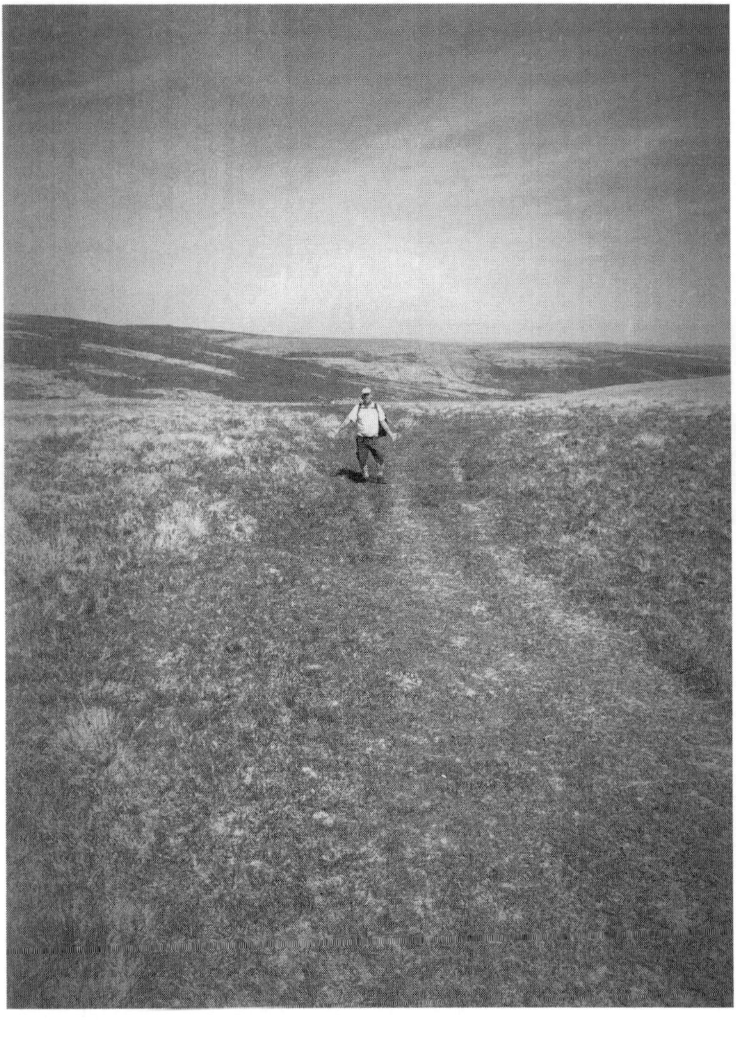

Sunday 21st

I awoke at seven to the gentle tone of the alarm on my phone, blearily pushed the duvet to one side and tottered over to the window to peer with squinted eyes at the carpark below. It was going to be hot – shorts would be the order of the day. Waking myself up properly by making a coffee, then following that with a reasonable shower, livened me up enough to stumble downstairs to the beer garden with another coffee in hand. My legs still ached, and the soles of my feet remained sore, so I lay on one of the benches with my head at one end and my feet resting at the other, supping my coffee at an awkward angle. No-one was around and it was all very quiet. But then, of course, it was only a quarter to eight on a Sunday morning. As I sat in the bright, cool morning air, I thought Ivybridge was a nice town. It acquired its name, rather simply, from an ivy-covered narrow bridge over the River Erme. A painting of the 'Ivy Bridge' was undertaken, once again, by our recently acquired friend, J. M. W. Turner in 1813, and hangs in the Tate Gallery in London. The bridge was an important crossing-point over the Erme on the Plymouth – Exeter Road: not only for intrepid 16th century through travellers, but also for the collection and dispatching of products from the adjacent mills, which included corn, tin and ore.

Around 1830, The Sportsmans Inn itself was called 'The Grocer's Arms' by the owners, the 'Grocers' Company', who obviously didn't think creatively when it came to naming pubs. This apparently fickle group of individuals were originally known as the Guild of Pepperers, which became the 'Fraternity of Pepperers' and then finally 'The Company of Grossers of London' (although sounding like a group of deviants, it derived its name from 'a wholesale dealer buying and selling in gross'). The first owner / landlord was a certain Richard Lethbridge, but it wasn't until seventy years later, twenty years after Mr. Lethbridge had pulled his last pint, that an individual called George Packer, along with his wife Sarah, took on the tenancy of the Inn from the then owner Samuel Luscombe, a local bigwig. Soon after the Packers had their feet under the table, large signs were fixed to the front and sides of the building with the words 'Packer's Sportmans Arms'. The Inn was now easy to spot, and local papers of the time advertised the fact that the Inn catered for char-a-banc parties, which is where they now all stopped: a pretty good advertising strategy by the Packers.

I wandered into the breakfast section of the pub to find Lee already seated. He'd had a slightly disturbed night, as his bedroom was directly above the pub area where the music had been playing – I hadn't heard a thing. We mumbled pleasantries and, assuming we would walk off any calories consumed, we ordered the full fry-up. A return trip to the bedroom followed, where I adorned myself in my shorts, and the sweaty tee shirt I had worn from Wembury.

Around ten, we were out of the door of The Sportsman's Inn and turned left towards Fore Street, where we located a Morrisons store. Bottles of water were purchased – a two-litre one each, along with two 500ml bottles for me and another single one for Lee. I also purchased a box of cappuccino sachets – the box being discarded immediately - the sachets disappearing into the depths of my backpack. We crossed the road and headed into the Harford Road carpark adjacent to the River Erme, to ensure all was well with our packs. While I rearranged my belongings, Lee undertook a small piece of his 'video diary', by basically waving a long stick around, which had a camera on the top of it, and talking to no one in particular. After he had finished, I had a small turn in front of the camera, feeling slightly self-conscious as I did so, reiterating where we were, and lying through my teeth about 'how much I was looking forward to the day'. I didn't last long – Lee was far better at it than me. We commented on the historic mill turbine by the river (which looks like a snail), then turned and made our way through the short garden area and onto Harford Road.

Starting off, as usual, we encountered a long gradual hill, up past the Stowford Paper Mill and the Ivybridge Community College where, just for fun, the hill then became even steeper. I had to stop and catch my breath occasionally as I made it to the junction with Cole Lane, where Lee was waiting, looking as fresh as a newly picked apple.

'You alright?' he asked.

I croaked something unintelligible and crossed the road to continue up the seemingly endless hill. If the road hadn't been harsh enough on the soles of my feet, someone, somewhere, had come up with a brilliant idea and decided that the road we were on, (leading to Harford Moor and the boundary of Dartmoor National Park) shouldn't be tarmacked anymore. The smooth surface was replaced with a generous spread of loose chippings and angular stones. As there had been no rain, the muddy lane we were on was as hard as concrete. I felt the impact of the change of surface through my boots as I continued to lumber up the hill toward the moor. As we crossed over a railway line, I recalled, with some alarm, a recurring phrase in the 'Cicerone' guidebook: 'ascend sharply'. These words seemed to be a permanent fixture etched into just about every page.

We finally reached a gate at the top of the stony lane where Cicerone states 'you are rewarded with glorious views over the moor'. By this time of course, a river of forehead sweat had trickled into my eyes, almost becoming an extra membrane. With my temporary impaired vision, it was difficult to see anything, let alone anything glorious. For all I knew, I had missed seeing several naked sunbathers on my way up the hill. I propped myself against the gate, alternatively lifted my feet to ease the pain whilst pouring water over my head. After a minute, my vision was restored.

After passing through the gate, we were faced with a couple of choices: we could either carry on straight ahead on the 'low-level' route which eventually wound its way up onto the ridge separating Harford and Ugborough moors or, we could head right, straight uphill onto the ridge and turn left (north). We, and by that I mean Lee, decided it would be best to do an uphill slog first as the rest of it should be a breeze. I didn't particularly care at that moment, although it did make sense. And, if anything, the 'low-level' route was slightly longer and, I would still have to climb uphill to meet the ridge.

'I'll see you at the top,' Lee told me encouragingly.

I took copious sips of water and poured some more over my head. I looked in the direction of the ridge which Lee had already set off for. It was at this point I came up with a strategy for walking uphill. I would aim for certain targets and, with my head down staring at my boots, I would head towards the first of many. Targets could be anything – a large rock, a gorse bush, a clump of heather, a crossing of paths – anything at all. Even a dead body would do, although, in all probability, it would more than likely be my own. My strategy seemed to work – I even factored in the gradient - the steeper the climb, the less distance to my selected target. When I reached a target, I would stop, undertake a quarter turn left, stretch one leg several times, then the other, undertake another quarter turn left and repeat the exercise, then again and again, until I was finally back facing the way I intended to go. I found this slight break with stretches invaluable, as it gave me time to rest my legs in all manner of different directions, easing my painful calf muscles. Any onlookers probably assumed that I was leisurely practising my moves for an individual Hokey Cokey competition.

Halfway to the ridge I crossed paths with an amiable herd of cattle. They ignored me which I was grateful for, as I usually attract them for some reason. Initially they come to visit me with curiosity but invariably end up becoming menacing. Hence my gratitude. I didn't have any energy to run anywhere and, if I did, there was nowhere to run to.

Lee was out of sight by this time, as I continued my slow progress up the hill. The sun shone intensely: it was getting warm, and I was getting hot. I was glad I only had on a tee-shirt and shorts, but a faint steamy mist was already beginning to appear from them. Near the top I left the 'track', which was really just a pathway of flattened grass made by countless walkers, and veered slightly left, forging my way through uneven ground which, although I was cutting a corner, the terrain was much more difficult, with uneven ground strewn with large boulders and clumps of gorse which needed circumnavigating. But eventually I made it onto the track on the ridge and sat down on a large boulder looking back on my uphill journey. I could still see the gate that I had passed through, way off in the distance. I felt quite pleased with myself – I had just conquered Butterdon Hill. It was breezy on the ridge, pleasantly so, as the sun had become more intense. I drank some water and rested until Lee appeared from my right a couple of minutes later.

The track we were on was 'The Red Lake Railway' (aka 'Tramway') - a narrow gauge mode of conveyance - which was built in 1910 or 1911, (depending on which book you read) to carry supplies and workers between Bittaford and the clay workings at Red Lake. Along the side of the track, piles of rocks, cairns and marker posts were evidence of a long-ago industry. Adjacent flooded pits and bridges also adorned the route. I wondered what it must have been like for the workers – the word 'awful' sprung to mind. And how about before the tramway (?) – the delivery of the ore must have been undertaken by horses and carts. I guess the guys who worked there must have been fit and tolerant of extreme conditions, particularly when winter set in. And also, on a day like today, extremely hot and sunny. All for a wage that might have bought them some ale and a lump of bread.

The track itself was undulating but had no serious ascents or descents for the next couple of hours. It was hard underfoot however, which brought further agony to the soles of my feet. With Lee a few hundred yards ahead of me I trudged along, staring at the barrenness of the whole area. I felt small in the immense landscape – it makes one think: which is a good thing. Good for the soul and all that. Time to think. Time to think about nothing and everything. Time to think about how bright and hot the sun was. Time to think about how hot my neck was becoming. I turned my baseball cap back to front so that my neck would be protected, but of course by that point the damage had already been done.

Three hours ensued as we laboured along separately, while the burning sun behind us cast small shadows on the track in front of us. Other walkers were also wandering around on the moor – at one point a runner came swiftly towards me and vanished over my left shoulder. I hated him. The fit git. I was struggling placing one foot in front of the other – at each step I questioned myself why I was doing it. Paul's voice filtered back into my mind: 'It's a walk Chris, enjoy it.' I recalled a similar incident with fit people in my life from thirty years previously. I had managed to scale Scafell Pike in the Lake District with a group who portrayed differing levels of fitness. As I draped myself in a fatigued state against the pile of stones with a metal plaque indicating the summit, a group of twenty fell runners came racing up to the top, slapped the plaque, and ran off back down again. I would have thrown rocks at their departing images if I'd had the strength. But at that point I was completely out of energy from rolling a cigarette.

A little further along the track, a couple of lads on quadbikes came whistling along, rudely interrupting our personal silences, like a shrill alarm clock breaking a dream. As they passed us, loose stones hurtled into the air. We continued along the ridge, passing easy to imagine places such as 'Piles Hill', and 'Left Lake', which, to me, were just physical anomalies in a predominately desolate landscape of large, brown mounds.

I caught up with Lee at a point I called 'the middle of nowhere in particular', and we checked the guidebook. We noted a convenient rest point not too far ahead - denoted as 'tin workings'. As my focus was slightly blurred by a combination of a covering of sweat, mild heatstroke and degenerative myopia, I read it as 'Tim Workings'. Lee and I, both having the same sort of odd humour, coupled with a small degree of sunstroke, proceeded to invent 'Tim Workings' as the lead in a fictitious combo trio that played in northern nightclubs. 'Ladies and gentlemen, please welcome to the stage, 'Tim Workings and the Tim Workings Trio!'

As we rested for about twenty minutes at 'Tim's place', I surveyed the bright red areas about my person. I could feel my skin tightening, like a cork into a bottle. The backs of my legs were fairly well cooked, and my arms up to my shoulders had taken on the colour of a freshly immersed lobster. As I turned my head from side to side my neck made a noise like a bag of crisps. My mouth felt arid, like it was coated in a fine sand. Lee checked the football games on his phone. Manchester City were beating Chelsea, and Brighton were beating Southampton. Most importantly, West Ham were beating Leeds United – I smiled at this news (I had placed a bet the previous summer on Leeds to be relegated: the day's win for West Ham placed another nail in the Leeds coffin: a few weeks later Leeds were relegated, and I collected my winnings).

After our break we continued north and past a path to Red Lake, the area of viable mineral wealth that had instigated the idea of the Red Lake Tramway. A little further on, the path swung right to face east – a section called 'Abbots Way'. Our path was along the top of a ridge; the gaze to our left was met by a wide valley dotted with clumps of heather and wandering sheep, with a tumbling stream at the bottom. It actually looked quite pleasing and was a marked difference to the blandness of the moor which we had recently crossed.

The guidebook directed us to make for a crossover point on the stream: we were confident we could see it from where we were, but we were in error. With our minds full of confidence, and moderately impaired by dehydration and mild sunstroke, we both stepped off the track and headed down the steep descent to the stream. The scale of the environment was such that the stream was much further away than we thought, and the descent was steeper. The ground underfoot was boggy, and several times I sank into it to the point where water-soaked mud made its way into the tops of my boots. There were also clumps of heather and gorse to navigate, as well as the customary large boulders. Lee veered off to my right as I headed directly downhill, scattering sheep as I went. I arrived at the stream – it was much wider than I had anticipated. I picked my way along its boggy edge until I became impatient and decided just to go for it. The stream, although fairly shallow, was crossed at the cost of wet feet, but there was a bonus that the mud, having adhered itself to my footwear, was conveniently washed away. Lee was more sensible, and continued to walk along the stream's edge until a far easier crossing point was noticed and undertaken. When we were both safely across, we compared wet boots and then looked at the Cicerone guide. 'To stay on the two moors proper, do not head down directly into the valley' it stated. Oh well.

I dunked my baseball cap into the stream and slapped it onto my head which had an immediate cooling effect. Catching me out slightly, the excess water ran down my back which made me stiffen up, ending in a stance that looked like I had forgotten the next move in my Hokey Cokey practice. Lee gave me a strange look – I couldn't blame him. Once I became mobile again, a little further on we found the clapper bridge by which means we were meant to have crossed. We followed the stream, crossed another clapper bridge and, at the same time, failed to notice a left-hand fork which led to a place called Hickaton Hill. By doing this we overshot the Two Moors route again and ended up heading toward a large lake.

'Is this right?' I asked Lee. Out came the guide again.

'No,' he responded.

We reread the guide, backtracked a quarter of a mile, and set off up the correct path. Hickaton Hill was conquered, and we found ourselves on a small part of Buckfastleigh Moor.

Very quickly we started to descend toward the village of Scorriton which I thought would be fine, as the backs of my legs were aching from all the days uphill work. But the body is a fickle thing. The descent was steep, which aroused the muscles at the front of my legs: it was their turn to become painful. As my feet were numb from the earlier unforgiving tramway, I failed to glean any benefit from the grassy downhill path, which was actually quite soft underfoot. It felt like I was walking on an expensive, green carpet. We weaved through outbursts of gorse and small hawthorn trees until we reached a crossing point over the River Mardle: a small bridge at a location called Chalk Ford. We remembered our odd humour that we had conjured up with the invention of 'Tim Workings' – 'Chalkie Ford' became the compere of our fictitious northern nightclub. 'Here's your host – Chalkie Ford!!' We had obviously been walking around on the moor in full sunshine for long enough that day.

I sat down by the bridge and peered at the other side, espying our route which took on a sharp incline through some woods. The muscles in the backs of my legs were about to be assaulted again. I decided I would rest up for ten minutes while Lee forged ahead with a customary 'see you at the top!' There wasn't much further to go that day, and a cool beer awaited just over the other side of the hill at a place called 'The Tradesman's Arms'. But it could wait ten minutes. I sat by the gurgling River Mardle in the late afternoon, with the sunlight filtering its way through the overhanging trees and onto my face. It certainly was a restful place and extraordinarily peaceful. I liked it very much.

But now it was time to finish the walk for the day. I swung my backpack onto my shoulders, gritted my teeth and made my way up the hill through the woods. After passing through three gates, I arrived at the top. Lee was in the distance and shouted at me 'see you at the bottom!' In front of me was a descending lane of a mile or so, and its surface was exactly the same as the one those idiots had made on the walk up to Harford moor earlier that day: a lane 'paved' of loose, sharp, large stones. The reawakening of the muscles on the fronts of my legs coincided with the pain receptors on the soles of my feet awakening from their slumber, just in time for me to obtain the full benefit of painfully picking my way along a steadily descending lane. Agony doesn't come anywhere near it.

Lee was the bottom of the lane waiting.
'Nearly there,' he said, and pointed left along the road. 'Not far. Just around the corner'.
He wasn't lying. After another few minutes we found ourselves standing outside the Tradesman's Arms pub where a lager shandy, followed by a meal, awaited. The pub itself almost closed in 2008 but was saved by four regulars who bought it – I guess we were fortunate in this respect, as there would have been nowhere to get anything to eat.

Officially, the route at this point urges a stopover in the small village of Holne, but accommodation is extremely limited and fairly hit and miss. I could have booked us into the Tradesman's Arms: at the time of organising things, I was unaware if there was any accommodation there. There was. But at the time I had decided to go a bit fancy and had booked us into a Shepherd's Hut at Michelcombe, on a site called 'Dartmoor Shepherd Huts' – a bit of a glamping site. This was about a mile away from where we were drinking ice-cold lager shandies in a sunny beer garden. The short journey to our overnight stop could wait – for now, it was kicking back time while we decided what to eat. It didn't take long – I was going to stick to another pie and chips. But instead of the previous evening's 'steak and ale', tonight would be 'chicken and mushroom'. Lee opted for a burger.

While waiting for our meal, we chatted to a couple in their early sixties I would guess. They were quite pleasant and were also undertaking the Two Moors Way: today they had undertaken the same route as us, having walked from Ivybridge. When I say I chatted, I really meant that I moaned at them with my tales of sore feet and aching muscles. The woman giggled – she thought I was performing a comedy routine. When I added the pain of my sunburn into my monologue she was pretty much in hysterics. Lee rolled his eyes as I wailed and whinged about how much my feet and legs ached. The food arrived and my whining subsided. The woman wiped her eyes.

'Thanks,' she said, 'you're so funny, and your stories really cheered me up'.

'You're welcome' I grumbled, and set about demolishing my pie.

Dammit! The ale had been drunk, and the food devoured. So now we had to head off to our accommodation for the night, unlike the easily amused woman, who was obviously into *schadenfreude*, and her husband, who were staying at the pub. Grudgingly, I pulled my backpack on and wandered back onto the road with my gnawing leg muscles and smarting feet, which had been in the belief that the day's work was over. Not a bit of it. Lee and I walked along the road into the hamlet of Michelcombe, about fifteen minutes away.

We found the 'glampsite' easily enough, and our shepherd hut. A quick bit of looking at previously sent emails from the owners, revealed a code for the key box hanging on the side of the hut. With the door unlocked, we dove inside to inspect our abode for the night. The two beds were of the bunk variety, and I immediately claimed the lower – I didn't have enough energy left to climb the small ladder to the upper. The hut itself was compact, but very satisfactory. The kettle was placed onto the gas stove in the kitchen area and the cappuccino packets were put to use. The hut had a wood stove inside (which we didn't bother using) and a shower / bathroom area, which we did bother using. It was all nicely self-contained and suited our purposes, plus it was totally different from a standard pub or hotel room. There was no television but that wasn't a problem. It was only nine o'clock, but I was ready to go to bed: again, being totally wiped from the day's exertions. I grabbed a cappuccino and went and sat outside on a rustic bench and rolled a cigarette. The light was beginning to fade rapidly, as I stared silently into the unlit firepit, which was also provided with the hut. Lee informed me that our distance that day was 13.9 miles; while we had been up on the moor the temperature had hit 23° degrees. I confessed that I had found the day very hard and if I had been attempting this on my own, and it had been raining, I probably would have quit.

Ten minutes later I fell onto my bed – Lee hoisted himself up the ladder and began to settle in the bunk above me. With his settling, the boards of the bed creaked alarmingly above my head, and I had visions of them snapping in half and Lee descending onto my prostrate body, flattening the last of my life force from me. I fell asleep to the sound of the bed-boards creaking.

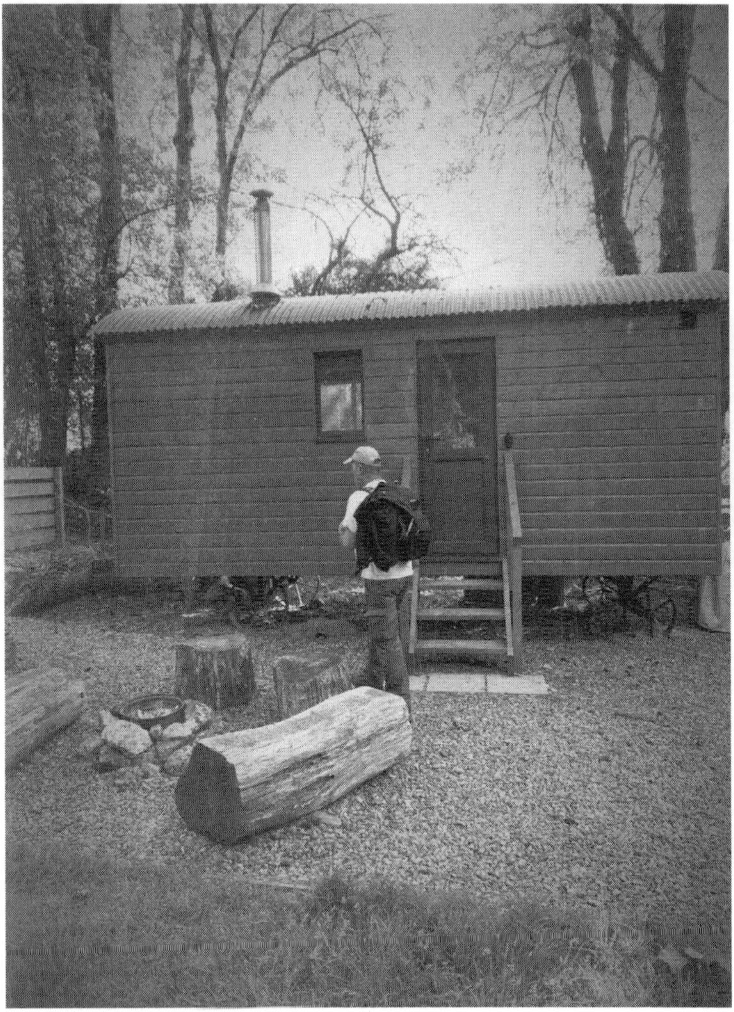

Monday 22nd

I awoke at six and ached all over. The kettle went on: five minutes later I was outside in the early morning sunshine with a cappuccino and a cigarette, inspecting the affected parts of my body for sunburn. From north to south, my neck, upper arms and the backs of my legs all sported a nice crimson shade. My leg muscles - back and front - ached. The soles of my feet were sore.

Lee awoke half an hour later and more cappuccinos were swallowed. We studied our maps and guides, tidied up our backpacks and planned the day ahead. A check on the stock of flapjacks revealed that there were twenty-four left. Lee had one with his coffee. It was shower time for me and a complete change in the underwear and tee-shirt departments. My previously worn garments would be binned somewhere, as they had performed their duties for the last time. I sat outside, dined on a flapjack and waited for the off, while Lee took on the shower.

After a perfunctory cleaning of the shepherd's hut, we set off for Holne along Michelcombe Lane: needless to say, it was uphill. At the top we meandered our way through an area called Play Cross and then through the village of Holne. Conveniently, a roadside waste bin was ready and willing to accept my recently divorced clothing. We walked past the 'World's Smallest Pottery Shop' (how do they know this?) and continued northwards until we found ourselves on a footpath which ran alongside the righthand side of the River Dart. The area was fetchingly scenic and the river melodic and cooling, as the bright sun encouraged the temperature to ascend higher. Walking in a reverie with sunlight glinting from the river was an uplifting experience. The aches from my body were beginning to disappear, and any pain from sunburn was similarly dissipating. I actually felt good. I think my mindset had changed completely.

We emerged onto a road (Newbridge Hill) at New Bridge: a slightly ironic name as the bridge, made from local granite, was built in the 15th Century. We made our way up Newbridge Hill for a short while, before the road swung left and we stepped onto a footpath on our right to track alongside the River Dart again. We walked along an enchanting riverside meadow in the bright sunshine for approximately half a mile before taking a small lane, which wound its way uphill away from the river for about a mile, to the hamlet of Leusdon. Although a slightly taxing hill, the scenery somehow made things marginally easier, with undulating meadows and moorland on both sides of us, as we were contained within small stone walls and hedgerows. I began to notice some of the wildflowers which were in abundance: I'm no botany expert, but the hedgerows were rampant with a mixture of cow parsley, red campion, ragwort, stinging nettles and an occasional dog rose. It was all rather beguiling.

Half a mile from Leusdon was the hamlet of Ponsworthy, which we briskly breezed through as it was all downhill, passing a 'fingerpost' named 'Forder Bridge'. We were to pass many fingerposts on our journey, most of them possessing names which I assumed denoted a local area, but some names were somewhat obscure. This post indicated 'Widecombe', (I guess there wasn't enough room on the 'finger' to fit in all of its proper name) as three miles further on. At the bottom of the hill, we crossed over the River Webburn and then found ourselves back on the Two Moors Way again, on a footpath which followed the river for a mile or so, before we crossed over it again at a place called Jordan Mill. Lee, who was wearing shorts, was stung several times by malicious nettles. By more luck than judgement, and to save my legs from further burning, I had opted for my combat trousers, so didn't suffer Lee's fate of being assaulted by small quantities of formic acid. But at least both sets of our legs would be red by the end of the day, albeit via different means.

The lane from Jordan Mill was now all uphill: we had benefitted from the walk down into the river valley and now it was time to 'pay the fiddler'. With breaths becoming sharper and legs becoming more strained, we traipsed to the top, then strode northwards in a purposeful manner along Manor Cottages and into Widecombe-In-The-Moor. As we passed The Old Inn on our left, we espied a heavenly vision. On the village green in front of us was a hut which was open, tended by a rotund, middle-aged woman with a broad mid-Devon accent, serving beverages and, on further enquiry, resulted in us being able to purchase sausage sandwiches. After nothing more than a flapjack for breakfast, it was tea for Lee, cappuccino for me, and two sandwiches were the order of the day. As we sat on the one of the few benches available and awaited our breakfast, I looked around me and took in the sights of the village.

Widecombe is thought to be a derivation of 'Withy-combe' which apparently means Willow Valley. The main income for Widecombe is from tourism, although as I looked around, I couldn't really see what it had to offer. Where we sat was just a car park, a tea shack, and a large bin on wheels. And the bin was locked. I guessed that

Widecombe Fair with its accompanying folk song were the lure for most tourists. Literally towering over us was a church known as 'Cathedral of the Moors', although its real name is the Church of St. Pancras. This sort of pleased me: as a child I was raised in Central London and my school, Argyll Infants and Juniors, was across the Euston Road from St. Pancras station. I turned my gaze to the road and noticed a flyer nailed to the fence advertising a mammoth event for Widecombe. The flyer encouraged all to come and see, 'for one night only', 'The Squeezy Geezers'. I can only assume that accordions would be involved.

'Let's get out of here before they turn up,' I said to Lee.

'But Chalkie Ford might be introducing them!'

I mused.

'Perhaps the Tim Workings Trio are also playing?'

Lee squinted at the fence. 'Nah. They're not on the flyer.'

As we sat there joking with each other, a woman wandered past with a lad of about thirteen. The woman was looking for somewhere to dump an armful of rubbish she was carrying and aimed straight for the large bin on wheels. Lee and I watched in childish glee as her facial expression changed from one of triumph in finding a bin, to exasperation and despair on finding the bin locked. With our amusement satisfied with the woman, we turned our critical eye onto the young lad. I looked more closely at him and noticed that his hair on one side of his head was completely shaved off. The other half of his head was covered in thick, long hair which not only covered his neck, but for some strange reason he had decided that his hair needed to be combed over from right to left (in a classic Bobby Charlton manner) thereby covering some of the shaved area.

'I really hope his name is Bobby,' I muttered to Lee, who laughed.

'Why didn't he just keep his hair?' I asked.

'It's fashionable' replied Lee, but I could see he was as taken aback as much as I was, to the point where he secretively took a short video of the lad and sent it my daughter-in-law with a whispered voiceover saying, 'Hey Maria, have a look at this kid's hair!'

Having recently retired from teaching, I am fully aware of all the current attention-seeking strategies undertaken by the younger generation. It must be admitted however, that I used to do similar things along with my own generation, which just followed trends set by previous ones. As teenagers, we all had statements to make. What we didn't do was attempt to confuse everyone by trying to change into different identities, or genders come to that. I can only assume that the lad with half his head shaved wasn't too sure as to what he should identify as. It's possible he was close to making a definitive decision but was rudely interrupted and forced to accompany his parents to Widecombe-In-The-Moor for the day.

Feeling better after a more normal breakfast, we decided it was time to hit the road. The woman from the tea shack came to clear away bits and pieces from our table and asked us where we were going.
'Lynmouth' I responded.
'But today,' added Lee, 'Chagford'.
'Well, oi've just 'erd on the wharless,' our saviour in sandwiches and drinks said, 'you should keep an oi out for a Red Koite up on the moorrr'.
'Any strings attached?' I quipped. She stared at me puzzled.
Lee saved any further embarrassment. 'We'll keep an eye out for it,' he said.

As we walked out of Widecombe, many adverts and flyers adorned fences and walls suggesting that Widecombe-In-The-Moor was indeed a 'must-see place'. I couldn't quite understand it. What I had seen was a shop selling general tourist tat which was closed, a pub which was closed, a church which was shut, a tea shack, a gravelled carpark with a locked bin on it and a kid with a strange hairdo. I questioned why anyone would really come here unless the Fair was in town. Still, each to their own. At least we got away before 'The Squeezy Geezers' appeared.

The road out of Widecombe led us past a tennis court and onto a lane called Bronze Road: I raised an eyebrow to a road sign on our right, which thanked us for 'taking 'moor' care'. As difficult as it was to stifle our mirth, we pressed on up a fairly gentle incline until the road levelled out. Wooder Manor Holiday Homes appeared on our left, then quickly vanished behind us as we marched down a small hill, veered right, and crossed the East Webburn River. After the crossing, the road, the East Webburn Way, gently rose through a picturesque woodland which was intoxicating to walk along: there was little sound - a gentle breeze disturbed the trees; birds, concealed from us, warned everything in the woods that we were about. Looking back on it now, it was one of my favourite sections of the whole journey.

Halfway to the top of the hill, we passed a gated establishment called Bagpark I was pleased once again – it reminded me of a television program called 'Bagpuss'. The 'Dartmoor Coach House' appeared next on our left, with its manicured gardens falling away to the river below, which was overshadowed by Hamel Down on its far side. The woodlands thinned out on either side of the road, and we were left with views of meadows all around us. The road was bordered by a moderate hedgerow on our right accompanied by the customary range of wildflowers. To our left, a small stone wall, which must have been at least two hundred years old, was covered in mosses and ferns. I noticed a small herd of alpacas in a meadow as we passed Pitton Farm: as I had been walking along, I had wondered what could be farmed around this area. Apart from a small flock of sheep here and there and a couple of lonely cows, most of the meadows appeared to be devoid of animal life. It's no small surprise I suppose that most farms have converted outbuildings into 'holiday cottages' to source an income. We stopped for ten minutes at a cattle grid to chomp on another flapjack, washing it down with water. It was extremely quiet, and I liked it very much.

The road descended past Isaford Farm, over a stream of miniscule dimensions, and then began to rise again, but by now my body was getting used to such things. My new mindset was still working; I'm not saying I found the going easy, but it was certainly becoming 'doable'. The soles of my feet apparently now possessed the property of iron: there was no pain at all, and I could hardly feel anything through my boots. I was definitely feeling much improved, in both mind and body. Preoccupied with these thoughts, I absent-mindedly stumbled into Lee, who was waiting for me at the top of the hill next to a gate.

'Have a look at this fella Dad,' he motioned, with a wave of his hand. Standing about ten yards away from the gate was a huge bull.

'Jeez,' I responded. I'd never seen a bull so large. 'He's a big lad'.

'I bet he keeps the ladies happy,' commented Lee.

'If he doesn't crush them first.'

'Well, they'd probably die with a smile.'

'Anything flattened by that would look like they were smiling.'

Lee nodded in agreement. The bull eyed us as we wandered off along more hedgerow-bordered lanes, with occasional gaps between overhanging trees, permitting more views of high moorland areas rising up on either side of us. Behind us the view was spectacular.

We passed a sign on our left which read 'Karuna Institute'. Both Lee and I were curious to know what the property was used for, and we discussed the matter whilst resting at the top of a hill in predominately open moorland, next to a sign which indicated we were close to Heathercombe Woodlands.

'I think it might be a retreat of some sort,' I ventured. Lee wasn't so sure.

'I reckon they do weird experiments on demented people in there.'

I mumbled something in response, incoherently, as I forged my way through another flapjack. It wasn't until after our walk that I checked it out on the internet: 'a UKCP accredited professional training in Mindfulness Based Core Process Psychotherapy and Relational Mindfulness Trainings.' So, in a way, neither of us were correct. But in another way, both of us were.

Our journey led us downhill through more dense woodlands, with a sprinkling of road signs indicating 'children'. In some consternation, I wondered what on earth children were doing out in this remote area of nowhere. But all was revealed a quarter of a mile down the hill, as we shambled passed the Heatree Activity Centre. My consternation was eased.

After another quarter of a mile, we arrived at a crossroads where a sign informed us that by turning left, Chagford was five miles away. Annoyingly, the sign to our right let us know that after all our wanderings since our sausage sandwiches, Widecombe was only four miles behind us. I drank some water and resignedly followed Lee along the road guarded by tall hedgerows and wildflowers for just over two miles, accompanied by the presence of King Tor on my left. The hedgerows became overshadowed by dark woodland for a while: I could see a pinetum immediately behind the deciduous trees on my left, and I considered that to be another way of using the land. Moorland aside, there were abundant meadows which I assumed belonged to the sporadic farmhouses we passed. But there didn't seem to be any farming going on – I wondered if most of the farmhouses were now the property of people wealthy enough to just buy a spread with a nice view of Dartmoor and enjoy life. Or whether the farms we passed were still working. I wasn't about to go and knock on doors, so I guess I'll never know.

We arrived at the junction of the B3212, at a sweeping bend. Emulating it, we swept ourselves right, passing a few ancient-looking beech trees then, after a hundred yards or so, swept ourselves left into another small lane which set us due north, or thereabouts, to Chagford. We had just passed a couple of houses by the roadside which meant we had travelled through an area called Batworthy. If we had blinked, we would have missed it completely.

Our little used lane, which had grass growing in the middle of it, reminded us of many similar lanes we had previously trodden. More pleasant views were encountered as we ambled our way along separately. It was nothing personal between myself and Lee: there was just no need to walk side by side. My feet were just commencing to ache anew, and I realised again, although much too late in the day, that for walking along roads, walking trainers were, without doubt, the better option. I had nothing but my large, heavy boots, whereas Lee was definitely the more comfortable out of the pair of us. I consoled myself with the fact that my boots were probably best suited to the moorlands and anything else 'off-road' as it were. But the trek across Dartmoor itself, with its rock-hard terrain, had meant that walking trainers reigned supreme there also. I made a mental note to buy some trainers.

The sun was high, and the temperature continued to creep up during the afternoon, reaching 23° as we slowly made our way toward our accommodation for the night. It wasn't a lot further, I told myself. Sheltered and cooled slightly by overhanging trees, we crossed over another small stream – its murmurings suggesting I put my feet up for five minutes. I acceded. Up another hill, passing more lanes on our left and right, we continued roughly northward until a sudden downhill section was encountered. Far ahead in the distance we could both see more hills of Dartmoor. But the middle distance interested me more at this point. In front of me, at the bottom of the hill, was Chagford. Soon I would be able to rest my feet again. But prior to that, I would have to ensure that some resting leg muscles, in particular the ones I only used when walking down steep hills, would now have to come into action.

At the bottom of the hill, we tiptoed over a cattle grid: a good sign that we were entering a town. The environment changed abruptly from one of moorland and quietness, to one of houses and cars. The houses on the right-hand side of Meldon Road, where we now walked, looked like council houses which had been purchased. The views from their front rooms and bedrooms directly overlooked the moor on our left and must be a pleasant sight to wake up to each morning. Meldon Road became New Street for some strange reason, but that didn't last long as, at the church, St. Michael the Archangel to be exact, the road became the High Street. We walked past the Globe Inn and the Three Crowns until we finally reached our destination selected by Lee: the Ring O' Bells pub, just by the market square in the middle of town.

We clattered our way inside the pub which had one customer. The barmaid was an attractive thirty something, but she looked wiry and strong, and gave an air of an individual who didn't put up with any nonsense in either her work or personal life. She booked us in, and we went upstairs to dump our backpacks, returning promptly for two lager shandies and a meander out to the beer garden at the rear of the property which, in all reality, was a converted back yard, but converted reasonably well enough. We chatted to another couple who were on the Two Moors Way proper and heading off to Morchard Bishop in the morning, as the guidebook dictated. As I didn't have too much to whine about, I was less funny in conversation: or maybe they didn't have a sense of humour. Or maybe my sense of humour had left me. My red legs were cooling to a light brown, and the crisp packet effect I had felt on my neck, had just about run its course. My legs still ached of course, and the soles of my feet were, after the day's efforts, a bit painful; tomorrow I would wear two pairs of socks, which I was sure my feet would welcome. A shower before dinner, then another pie and chips for me (a plain steak one this time). Lee also partook of this wonderful walker's fare. Two more ales apiece, and we tottered of to our separate rooms which overlooked the market square. Around half-nine I telephoned Kirsty, and then dozed to the television set, feeling fairly content. Another fifteen miles had been covered today and tomorrow would be the midpoint of our journey.

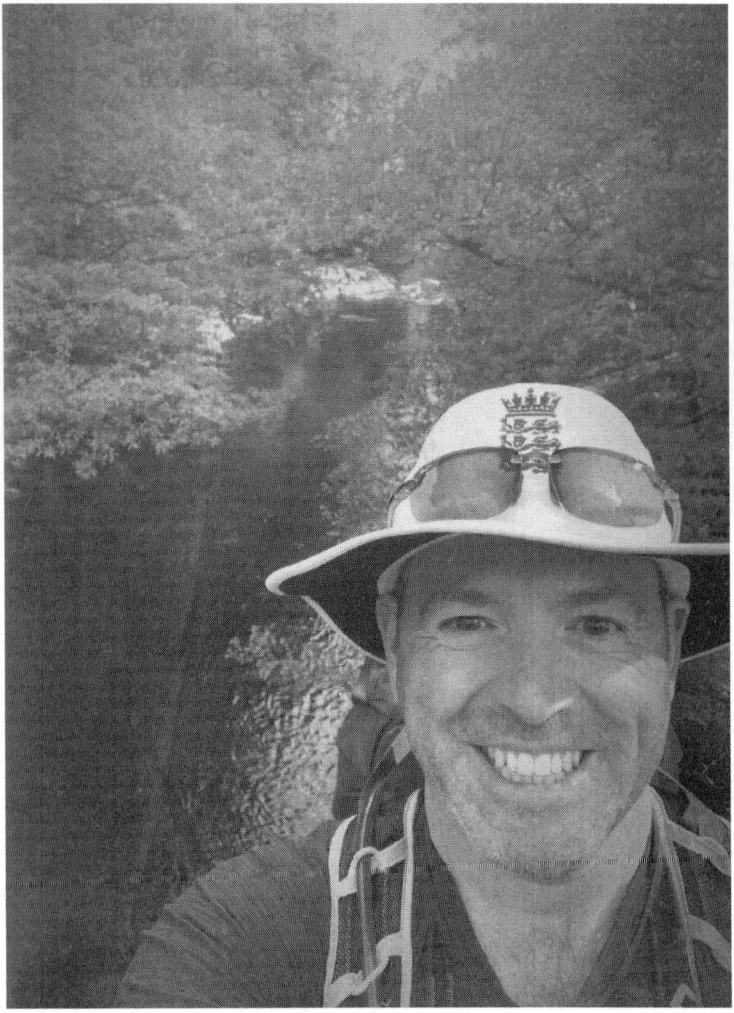

Tuesday 23rd

I was awake around seven and immediately dived toward the kettle. A cappuccino sachet was torn asunder, and the contents sprinkled into a cup. I adorned myself with what I considered a reasonable amount of clothing, finished rolling a cigarette at the same time the kettle indicated that it had boiled by a loud click, and wandered downstairs and out of the side door which led to the beer garden. It was chilly – the early morning sunlight was on the other side of the building, so I traipsed back the way I had come, past the side door and out into the street. I crossed the road and headed for a bench which was in full sunlight, and faced the pub.

After a few minutes, a girl (in her twenties I would guess) sat next to me and a short conversation was struck between us. She was off to work. I was off to walk. A bus pulled up, she boarded, and ten seconds later I was back alone with my thoughts. I looked about me. There were a few shops around the market square and along the high street, but there didn't seem to be enough employment opportunities to satisfy the whole working community. I made a guess that some people would commute to either Exeter or Okehampton.

I quite liked Chagford, even though further research revealed that a study in 1987 discovered high levels of Radon gas in the surrounding area of granite, resulting in a claim that Chagford contained the most radioactive toilet in the world. Peering deeper into Chagford's secrets, I read with interest that during the Civil War, a Royalist, Sidney Goldolphin, was shot and killed in the doorway of the Three Crowns pub I had walked past, and the churchyard contains a memorial to a certain Mary Whiddon, who was shot dead as she walked out of the church on her wedding day (I could see a theme developing here). Evelyn Waugh stayed at the Easton Court Hotel and wrote Brideshead Revisited, but I don't think he shot anyone while he was doing it.

I wandered back inside the pub and up to my room, showered and got dressed. I went to breakfast *sans* boots, but wore two pairs of hiking socks. The soft feel of the carpet under my feet was bliss. After another hefty fry-up, Lee and I returned upstairs to pack our possessions away and to prepare ourselves for the day. In addition to my fresh, two pairs of socks, I also squeezed myself into a clean tee-shirt and underwear. The previously worn-out items were placed religiously into a carrier-bag and ceremoniously dumped into a waste bin in the market square. I pushed my feet into my boots, and they did feel more comfortable. Lee, not being as wasteful with his clothes as I, wrapped his dirty laundry up in a parcel, went along the High Street to the Post Office and mailed them back to Kirsty. I made a mental note to call Kirsty and tell her not to open any parcels which might arrive over the next day or so. I threw my backpack on, sauntered downstairs and while Lee was in the Post Office sending hazardous materials through the mail, I went into a shop called James Bowden and Son, 'Hardware and Moorland Centre', and purchased an ordnance survey map, Number 113, which covered Mid-Devon, as we were going to be a considerable distance from the Two Moors Way. Lee had booked us a room at a place called The New Inn at Colebrooke, which was northeast of us, but we had decided we were going to put in a distance today, and head just about due north to a town called Lapford. At Lapford station we could catch a train back to Copplestone, then a taxi the short distance to Colebrooke. The following morning, we would do the reverse – it certainly wasn't cheating - in fact we would cover more miles today: tomorrow, we would merely pick up from where we had left off, ie Lapford.

Lee reappeared from the Spar shop which housed the Post Office, adorned with more bottles of water. We left Chagford at about a quarter past ten and headed out north along the B3206, past some antiques shops and a bakery along Southcombe Street, which changed into Lower Street. Strangely, and contrary to our normal experiences first thing of a morning, there was no 'steep ascent' but an easy downhill stroll. My double sock strategy felt great, and I could hardly feel a thing under my feet. I bounced along in a light frame of mind, as Lower Street continued to descend gradually into what could only be another river crossing at the bottom, where we would then be faced thereafter with another toil up another large hill. Still, might as well make hay, as they say. We reached a signpost, where to venture straight on would lead us to Moretonhampstead; the left fork lane signposted to 'swimming pool' was the one for us. We wandered down the hedge bordered lane past a couple of farmhouses, and crossed the delightful River Teign over a small, stone road bridge.

With flood meadows either side of us, we walked up a small gentle incline and found ourselves at the Chagford swimming pool. Two fairly stout women of advancing years, who were obviously walkers, (being adorned with large backpacks) were lamenting the fact that the pool wasn't open. As we passed them, I said cheerily, 'there's always the river back there.'

Both turned toward me sharply; one of them hissed, 'We know.'
I was a bit taken aback. I was only trying to a have a small joke with them. I reconciled myself to the probability that, in order to take on lots of extra calories, they had decided to unburden themselves of a sense of humour to free up some more space.

A short walk away from the swimming pool, we rejoined the Two Moors Way again for a brief while, by turning onto a footpath at Rushford Mill Farm. A peaceful, scenic walk through a water meadow led us into a woodland, where we bumped into the couple I had chatted to the previous afternoon, in the beer garden of the Ring O' Bells. We acknowledged and nodded to each other and had passed them no further than twenty yards or so when we heard a cry behind us. The husband had walked into a low-hanging, sturdy branch, which had met his temple with a reasonable amount of force. Lee and I earnestly enquired if they needed any assistance. As he sat dazed on a fallen tree, the husband looked like he had nearly knocked himself out. Aside from this, and apart from the small rivulets of blood trickling down his face, they both assured us that all was fine. We pressed the matter a little, but further assurances were given. What do you do? He might have been concussed. But we'd offered help, and it had been declined so, fair enough.

We walked through the rest of the woodland, minding our heads as we went, until we arrived at the A382 at Dogmarsh Bridge. Straight across the road, the Two Moors Way continued into the Castle Drogo estate: we turned left and headed north once again, towards a place called Sandy Park.

For an A road, it was fairly quiet - I hazarded a guess that any commuters that used the road would now be sat at their workplaces in the rising heat. Long straights with intermittent wide verges allowed us to walk along this stretch relatively safely. In that moment, life felt good. A crossroads indicated Drewsteignton and Castle Drogo to our right, but we continued north through Sandy Park. After about a third of a mile, a small lane on our right forked away from the main road which veered off westward. Having avoided any confrontations with vehicles, we now found ourselves on a little used small road called Stone Lane, which ascended between high hedgerows and overhanging trees, shading us from the 20° heat. Head down, I trudged up the hill, conquering reasonable inclines without stopping, and using 'markers' for short rests when the incline became more testing. As before, my 'markers' were arbitrary depending on the steepness, and, of course, any intermittent stops were determined by whether or not I could be arsed.

A short distance past Stone Lane Gardens was a crossroads where we turned right towards Drewsteignton. This direction was fleeting: within a hundred yards we took a road left, to continue our northward journey towards and through a small remote area called Newton Barton. Small hedges allowed views of the surrounding countryside as we trudged up a short hill and down the other side, culminating, after around half a mile, in a rest stop by a small brook at the bottom. We sat for around fifteen minutes, swilling water into our dry mouths prior to an attempt on a flapjack. Slightly refreshed, we attacked the next uphill section, passing a farm, which appeared to occupy both sides of the road. It was at this point that I thought I could hear the noise of traffic. After another ten minutes of progress, with the noise becoming ever louder, the source revealed itself. We had reached the A30 dual carriageway and were just about to officially leave Dartmoor behind us. As our road veered right to run parallel with the A30 for a mile, I took a long, hard look back. The jumbled heaps of the Dartmoor tors remained ever present but had now receded a considerable distance.

Lee decided to have a break for a short while, so I sauntered on ahead. As I walked along, I was searching for a tunnel of some description which would allow me to safely cross under the main road to my left. The road was fairly flat and straight, and I assumed that it had once been part of the original A30. After half a mile or so, I saw a track leading off to my left and so headed onto it and found myself, in my haste, in a council yard of some description, used for dumping salt and gravel and suchlike. I retraced my steps and, a further half a mile later, I came to the end of the road where the tunnel was on my left. I walked through it, and I was out of Dartmoor National Park. A major milestone as far as I was concerned. We turned right onto Hask Lane and made our way along the wide grass verge. Some traffic flowed past us, but the main bulk of vehicles were on the dual carriageway about fifty yards away on our right. To my left, Hask Lane granted views across green rolling hills of mid to north Devon.

The road curved away from the main A30 then curved back again. Before a bridge crossed back over the dual carriageway, a signpost on our left informed us that we had found another section of the Two Moors Way. We walked through fields and meadows as the temperature rose even higher, ensuring we increased our perspiration rates. Just after a river crossing (the Yeo) at West Ford Farm, we left the Two

Moors Way again and headed northwest – by studying the map I was aware that this section was going to be somewhat testing, as it was just about all uphill out of the Yeo valley. Not only was it a long steep hill, but it was also one of those deceptive hills; just as you think you have reached the summit, a brow is reached, or a corner is turned, the hill just continues upwards as though it is in no mood to finish rising. As I rested from time to time, I would stare behind me and look again at the large brown mounds of Dartmoor through the haze.

After a hefty one-mile uphill walk, coupled with impressive views across the mid-Devon countryside, we stumbled onto a crossroads at a place called Hittisleigh, where we took a few minutes to catch our breath and glug copious amounts of water. We crossed the road and continued up the lane for another 100 yards or so until we arrived at a tee junction, where we turned right. The road was a single lane: one of those 'out of the way lanes', which appeared to be hardly used. Its main benefit was that it was fairly flat and was easy to walk along – why hadn't I bought trainers? Surrounding us were scattered fields containing scattered cows. We stopped by a gate next to Davylands farm for another short break, then continued on for another mile and a half through a patchwork countryside, bordered by low hedgerows either side.

We reached a road junction called 'Swallow Tree' (for some reason), straight ahead of us was our interim target of Bow and was indicated to be four miles further on. That was two hours in our money give or take. We pressed on over rolling hills: the lane once again appeared to be little used – it was almost possible to believe that the last vehicle to use it was a horse pulling a cart, fifty years previously. We stumbled onto another junction with the fingerpost proudly bearing the name 'Quince', (another obscure reference to something which only locals are allowed to know) with the finger pointing to Bow engraved with a '3'.

We were actually walking through a part of Spreyton Wood with more roadside wildflowers for company. Over another small brook and another tortuous hill to conquer followed. Lee was waiting for me at the next junction, which was called 'Hillerton'. Bow was still another two miles away. Lee and I chatted for five minutes as we consumed some more water, before he headed off to the next road junction where we would meet up again. I rolled a cigarette and watched him disappear into the distance. Ten minutes later, I followed Lee's footsteps and wandered along in a world of my own, again, thinking of nothing and thinking of everything. The silence was broken by two classically dressed gentlemen driving two classic cars, heading to Hillerton behind me: they were obviously reasonably well off enough to play around in vintage cars during midweek around country lanes. I crested a hill and could see Bow in the distance ahead of me. As I stopped and looked at the view, an old car, not a classic by any stretch of the imagination, with an even older gentleman pulled up beside me.

'Are you ok?' he asked.

'I'm fine, thank you' I replied.

'Do you need a lift?' he enquired. It was tempting, but I explained what I was doing and that my son was slightly further ahead. He seemed impressed and said he understood and waved goodbye. He was impressed with me. I could tell. He stopped again when he saw Lee.

'Is that your father back there?'

'Yes.'

'Well, I'm very impressed with him.' There you go. I told you he was impressed.

I caught up with Lee at the junction of 'Bow Station'.

'I'm really impressed with you' he joked.

We walked under the railway bridge and found ourselves on Station Road. After another half a mile of country lane smothered in overhanging trees, we arrived in the outskirts of Bow. As we progressed through to the A3072, we looked earnestly for a tearoom of some description, but there wasn't any. We ended up at the centre of the village, sitting on the corner of the A3072 eating flapjacks and drinking water, while lorries thundered past us kicking up dust everywhere, some of it settling on my head, some of it settling on my flapjack. I sat on the corner looking like a hobo, resting my feet on a drain, and thought, 'What a dump this place is.'

I wasn't wrong. Research into the village provided information that Bow is, in fact, considered to be a 'failed town', having been unable to attract enough trade to justify a status as a town. Even as far back as the mid-13th century, when Bow was granted charters for a weekly market and a three-day annual fair, an influx of people did not halt its decline and by 1850, Bow/Nymet Tracey was described as a 'small, decayed market town'. Even now, Bow offers limited wonders such as Mid Devon Caravans, a general store (Co-Op), and garden centre (Bow Garden & Aquatic Centre, 'with a Waterside Café'), a concrete company (Edworthy's Concrete), a doctor's surgery, and one public house. During the Civil War, Charles 1st stayed for one night when he was chasing the Earl of Essex into Cornwall. One night was probably more than enough for Charlie - we were definitely not going to stay that long. One good thing was the realisation that we were halfway through our walk, but the best thing that ever came out Bow, as far as I was concerned, were the roads leading away from it.

The noise was deafening, and the dust got everywhere. After ten minutes, we'd had enough. Picking ourselves up off the pavement, we headed first along Water Lane out from Bow, shedding dust as went. We passed through a small hamlet called Sutton, which was cloaked in peace and quiet, and also some more dust. I noticed, as we walked along, that the soil had taken on a dark red colour.

The fingerpost at 'Clapper' (where do they get these names from?) informed us that Copplestone was three miles to our right, but a place called Zeal Monachorum was less than a mile straight ahead. It was tempting to head for Copplestone, but we knew we would have a more arduous journey the following day if we did, so we continued on to Zeal Monachorum instead, knowing it was the last town before Lapford. The hope was, that once we arrived at Lapford Station, we might be able to rest for a short while before the train arrived at nine minutes past six. The next train after that wasn't due until a quarter past seven, so it wouldn't really matter if we missed our desired one, it would just mean an elongated rest break. We certainly didn't want to miss the later train as it was the last one of the day, which would have meant either an expensive taxi fare to Colebrooke, or an even more protracted rest break of roughly twelve hours, sleeping on a railway platform.

We pressed on, protected by woodlands on both sides, until we passed the sign indicating that we had reached Zeal Monachorum. The name of the village is a Latin translation for 'Cell of the Monks'; the manor had been given to the Abbey of Buckfast in 1018 by King Cnut (Canute), and the village itself is mentioned in the Domesday Book (1086). We passed another sign on entering the village proper: underneath the standard 30 mph sign was another one which read '20's plenty' – the town was obviously fairly safety conscious, and not concerning itself with the current temperature of 21º. In that respect, as far as I was concerned, '20' was also plenty. We ambled past a pub on our right called The Waie Inn, (I assumed it was named by someone from the northeast), then trooped up the hill to the Zeal Monachorum fingerpost positioned next to the churchyard, which is reputed to possess a 1000-year-old Yew tree. Our spirits were raised, not because we were next to a church, but because the fingerpost had Lapford indicated on it. Our target! And it was just shy of three miles. To us, that was an hour and a half walking time. What time was it? A quick check revealed it was half past four. We could do this! And get the six o'clock train to arrive at our accommodation, The New Inn, with time to rest and all would be great in the world. Babies would gurgle happily; kittens and puppies would play together, and mankind would finally achieve peace. We picked up the pace a small amount, with our believed renewed energy, and made our way through the rest of the village. Zeal Monachorum is a pretty village; totally opposite to Bow in just about all regards.

We continued roughly northward, heading for Lapford with a spring in our step. At the top of a hill, we espied our target in the distance, and another signpost informed us we had just over two miles to go. I thought about the train: would we make it in time? A mile of more rolling hills and peaceful lanes, with views of farmland stretching away into the distance were laboured through, before we crossed the B3220 at the Stopgate junction, with Winkleigh indicated to our left and Morchard Road to our right. We headed straight on along a narrow lane; Lapford was sighted at the bottom of the valley, as we walked down a section called Kelland Hill, finally reaching the A377. We turned in the direction of Barnstaple (I was starting to feel at home by this point, with all these familiar placenames), walked past a petrol station, (thinking we could obtain water there in the morning) and, after walking across a roadbridge over the railway, we arrived at Lapford station, stumbled down the steps and found ourselves on the platform next to the single track of the Tarka Line.

It was hard to believe that it had only been five days since I had passed through this station on my way to Exeter – it seemed like a lifetime ago. It was also hard to believe that it was bang on six o clock and there was nine minutes before our train arrived. It was a relief to know that we had made it. I took off my backpack and dropped it by my feet, slumped onto the stairs in the warm sunshine, and rolled and smoked another cigarette. The train arrived on time and, this being a request stop, Lee stuck out his arm and waved at the train, which slowly came to a stop. We bundled aboard for the one stop south back to Copplestone, arriving there after a few minutes. Lee then contacted a taxi firm which collected us from Copplestone station and delivered us outside the door of the New Inn in Colebrooke. Before entering our accommodation for the evening, we booked a taxi to pick us up the following morning.

The New Inn in Colebrooke I can heartily recommend. The room which Lee and I shared was huge, the bathroom was more like a ballroom and everything else was just about perfect. I sat in the beer garden and waited for Lee to reappear with our customary lager shandies.

While I waited, I glanced around me and noticed a sign which read 'when in the beer garden near the river, you must surprise your children'. A combination of myopia and a lack of refreshing alcohol were contributors to my error as, after a beer and a wiping of my eyes, on closer inspection the sign actually read, 'when in the beer garden near the river, you must supervise your children'. I dragged myself up to our shared bedroom, showered, undertook a quick foxtrot, and made my way back to the bar. No one was in there apart from the barmaid who, I guessed, was in her late thirties, and the two elderly owners who looked decidedly grumpy, probably because we were the only two people there. An hour later however, a lone hiker did materialise and stay for the night. This night for me was a gammon and chips undertaking - the gammon was beautifully cooked, about an inch thick, and as moist as my body on a fifteen mile walk in warm sunshine.

We retired to the beer garden around half eight, after the grumpy owners had told the barmaid to 'go and do something else', as she was obviously having too much fun chatting with us. I could tell she didn't really like working there, but it was obviously a necessity for her and her kids: she told us she had to journey in from Crediton each shift. Without wishing to stereotype, I had a feeling that she was probably a single mum, and doing her bit to make ends meet.

Around half nine, as the sun completely exited the beer garden, we did the same, and headed upstairs to slumber in front of the television. The beds were as comfortable as the room was spacious, which was welcomed: another 16.8 miles had been journeyed that day, and we were over halfway.

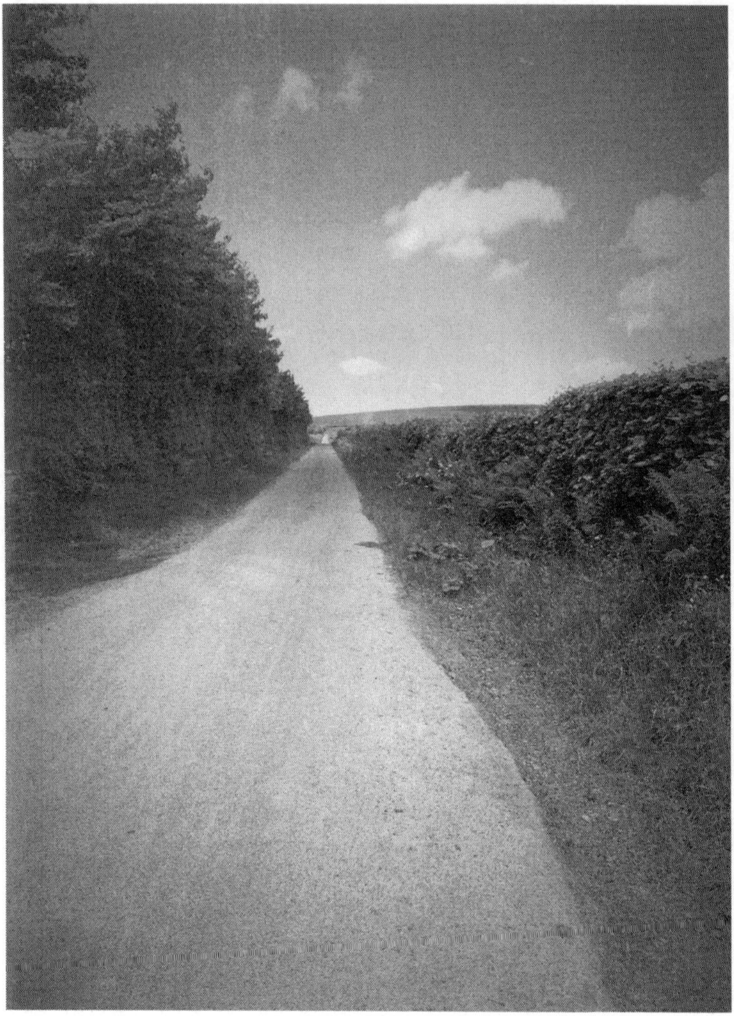

Wednesday 24th

Today was an earlier start than usual. Feeling well refreshed from a good sleep, and an evening of surprising small children, I alternated with Lee for the shower, and adorned myself thereafter with another fresh tee shirt and underwear, the previously worn items being dumped into a waste bin at Copplestone Station. A breakfast was dined upon in a hearty fashion, before we retired back to our bedroom to make the final adjustments to our packs. Organising duties undertaken, we returned downstairs, bade farewell, and jumped into our taxi, which arrived promptly at half past nine. The return trip to Copplestone Station only took a few minutes, so we waited on the platform in the sunshine (adjacent to the waste bin) for the train to take us back to Lapford, which also arrived promptly.

It was around ten o'clock when we reappeared at the top of the steps of Lapford Station and found ourselves back on the A377. As we had sufficient water on us, rather than go into Lapford itself, we turned left and walked along the road for about a hundred yards until we located a footpath on our right, just prior to a bridge over a very small stream. The footpath wandered uphill to the top of Lapford, so we did the same, arriving in Popes Lane.

It was quiet as we strolled along the road in the northern part of Lapford, with great views to our right of the rolling Devon countryside. We passed a small post office, and the church of St. Thomas of Canterbury, then stopped at a hall situated in a car park. The hall, manned by an elderly woman with a broad Devon accent similar to the 'Widecombe tea-lady', sold various provisions, but the only things we required were bottles of water which, we found in the fridge. Excellent. Ice-cold water would be useful as the temperatures were already beginning to rise. An adjacent fingerpost, identified as 'Orchard', informed us that we were three miles from Chawleigh.

After walking uphill for a time through the rest of Lapford, we soon found ourselves out in the countryside again, with green fields either side of us. The road was fairly level as we passed the 'Blackberry Lane Farm Shop', but then another hill had to be overcome as we made our way to a place called Forches Cross, where the fingerpost, rather unoriginally, was called 'Higher Forches' and informed us we had only walked half a mile from the previous one, which seemed a bit mean. A few yards further down the road, another fingerpost proudly bore the name 'Lower Forches'. I could only assume that there must have been an excess of wood in the area, so someone had decided to make a lot more fingerposts at every opportunity. The indication was that we were on the correct road to Chawleigh and Chulmleigh: to break up any feeling of monotony we might have had of open countryside views on a flat road, a moderate slope downhill led us over a small stone bridge and then back up the other side until we arrived at the B3042 at Leigh Cross. The fingerpost bore the name 'Labbetts', for some strange reason; I did try to make sense for some of the names on the fingerposts that we passed, but for this one, I drew a bit of a blank. The only reference I could find for the name was a bespoke bedroom furniture maker, based in Leicester: I would be straining credulity to even link them together. What the fingerpost did reference, was the fact that should we turn left, we would be one mile from Chawleigh. So we did.

After half an hour of relatively level walking, we gently descended into Chawleigh (twinned with St. Martin de Mailloc, they're proud to inform you): Chawleigh residents were also proud of the fact that they had been awarded 'the best kept village in 2002' – things could only have gone downhill since then. In the middle of the village was a fingerpost with 'Portsmouth Arms Cross' painted onto it next to a large pub – 'The Earl of Portsmouth'. I wondered what link there could be between a pub in the middle of Devon, and a city over one hundred and fifty miles away. It turned out that after a fire in 1869, the 5th Earl of Portsmouth, (born as Isaac Newton Fellowes, but resurrected the curious family surname of Wallop) who was a local landowner of a large estate a couple of miles to the west, helped to rebuild the pub. During its relatively recent history, the pub's name changed to 'The Portsmouth Inn' and then back to 'The Earl of Portsmouth'. The pub closed in 2019 for a year or so and then reopened. Sadly, it was closed, although not permanently, as we stopped to engulf large mouthfuls of water. As for Isaac Newton Wallop, he died at the age of 66 in 1891 after having fathered twelve children. I wasn't surprised. His wife died in 1906, probably of exhaustion.

A little further up the hill, as we made our way out of Chawleigh, a couple were sitting in a front garden of a house drinking cups of coffee. The house itself was a small shop cum café, where our enquiries rewarded us with a cup of coffee each. I smoked a cigarette, as Lee made friends with a small puppy which the guy was playing with. The women came out with our drinks and a conversation followed concerning our appearance in the village, and what we were doing there. The couple seemed relatively intrigued, (we don't get too many strangers round 'ere) but, overall, were just as happy to remain seated in the sunshine, drink cups of coffee, and play with a small dog. We waved goodbye – they were nice people.

At the top of the hill, a signpost directed us right onto the B3096 to Chulmleigh, which was a mile and a half away. I felt our journey was becoming easier by the minute: I felt good, and it had become a pleasure to stroll along through the soft undulating landscape. Although the scenery wasn't as dramatic as, say, the woodland bordered lanes in Dartmoor, or Dartmoor itself, it was certainly agreeable. As we headed down a hill towards the Dart River, a small lane appeared on our left, called Darky Lane. Hmm. I wondered what history was associated with this road, but with scant reference to it to be found anywhere, I can only surmise that it was so named because it was a sunken and heavily tree-lined dark lane, rather similar to 'Darkey Lane' found further west near Lifton.
We stopped and rested by the River Dart, which bubbled under the bridge cold and clear; two small trout went skittering into hiding as I leaned over the wall. A few minutes later we tramped our way up the appropriately named Chawleigh Hill: on our right, another lane peeled away – Egypt Lane. I could see a pattern developing here with ethnic minorities. I was almost right: Egypt Lane is presumed to have acquired its name

from gypsies, who themselves were presumed to come from Egypt.

Chawleigh Hill converted itself into Chulmleigh Hill which we conquered with much huffing and puffing. We wandered along Fore Street and sat on a bench by the Red Lion Hotel opposite a Spar shop and consumed another flapjack apiece. It was hot, and I made a mental note to go into the shop and purchase a bottle of fizz of some description, and down it before we set off again.

Outside the shop were a young couple with a toddler. All three looked decidedly unkempt: I know my personal attire at that point was akin to clothing that a refugee from a war-torn area would hesitate to wear, but the couple and their offspring took unkempt to a whole new level. The young parents, I assumed they were the parents, both looked as rough as a badger's crutch, and commenced a shrill shouting match with each other. A woman came out of the shop, spoke to the couple, picked up the toddler and disappeared back from where she had come from. The young couple picked up their argument from where they had left off, but mainly their discourse was a repeat of what had come before. I assumed there was a certain lack of eloquence from both sides and imagined that the only subject they were fairly informed on was how to fill in claim forms. In my reverie, I could see a worn-out sofa in their front garden. I snapped out of it when Lee stood up and announced he was going to the shop.

'I'll stay here and look after our stuff,' I told him, averted my gaze from the 'sparring couple', and looked around. The area looked fairly bland, with nothing going for it. It reminded me of Bow, and the difference I had found a short distance away in the village of Zeal Monachorum. The change from Chawleigh to Chulmleigh was decidedly similar, with a marked difference in apparent prosperity. Chulmleigh prospered well enough in the 17th and 18th centuries apparently, as it produced wool locally, offered a market and three annual fairs. The main road from Barnstaple to Exeter ran straight through the town. Unfortunately for Chulmleigh, during the 19th Century, a combination of wool production moving elsewhere, a turnpike road bypassing the place and the opening in 1854 of the North Devon Railway, all hammered nails into Chulmleigh's prosperity coffin. The decline of the town coincided with a decline in its population: in 2002 a census recorded the population at just over a thousand.

Lee returned from the shop and took my place guarding our backpacks. I wandered into the shop and purchased an ice-cold bottle of Dr. Pepper, which I demolished before my backpack went on. We headed up South

Molton Street: this was more like it - a street with a town name which I knew well. But that was as far as the likeable bit went; we walked past lots of small houses which, to be fair, looked fairly well-maintained, and a garage, but it really didn't look like much was happening. Maybe it was the fact that it was midweek in the early afternoon, and any other time of visit I would be met with a thrumming hive of activity. But somehow, I doubted it. It just seemed to me to be another dead town in the middle of nowhere. I couldn't begin to think where any work could be obtained: Barnstaple, Tiverton or Exeter I assumed. But all of these were probably around an hour away by bus. I couldn't think of many worse places to be at a loose end in – maybe a tower block in Brixton - it was all a bit depressing.

A right-hand fork by a huge dental practice at the top of the hill gave us a small shortcut toward South Molton. As we made our way out of the town, I was amazed to pass, in order, Chulmleigh Library, Chulmleigh Primary School and Nursery, Chulmleigh College PTA, Chulmleigh College, Chulmleigh Tennis Club and finally, the Chulmleigh Academy Trust. A vast number of resources and seats of learning for a town with such a low population. Perhaps they were expecting a baby-boom in the town. Maybe the young couple who were at odds with each other earlier could make a further contribution – after all, they must have agreed on at least one thing a couple of years previously. And, from what I had seen, there wasn't much to do in Chulmleigh apart from starting the process of contributing future learners.

At the top of the hill, I looked behind me and could still make out Dartmoor on the furthest horizon. It really did look a long way away behind us: had we really walked all that way? I looked ahead of me and, with a bit of a squint, thought I could just make out some distant hills of Exmoor, although I may have had something in my eye at the time: my eyesight had proved itself previously to be somewhat questionable. In terms of progress however, my personal journey was improving all the time. For the moment though, we were still in mid-Devon, with its undulating landscape, lanes with medium sized hedgerows, and remote farmhouses.

We stopped for a few minutes at Chulmleigh Beacon – there is a beacon there, a rusting cage atop a stout wooden post, about fifteen feet high. The road to our right was a route to the hamlets of Alswear and Meshaw, places I knew well enough as a friend lives there, just outside of the latter. Straight ahead, South Molton was six miles away. Full of determination, we strode forwards, passing 'Taw and Torridge' buses parked in laybys. These were also familiar to me, having seen them driving around in my local area, collecting and returning pupils to school. As we passed through Cadbury Barton, Exmoor was plainly visible ahead of us.

A long downhill stretch led us across a minute rivulet: a testing uphill section followed, but was made slightly easier halfway up, as some kindly soul had created a stone bench for me to sit on for ten minutes. Near the top of the hill, which seemed fairly endless, the 'Lightleigh Junction' fingerpost indicated Kings Nympton one mile; South Molton five. 'Two more hours or thereabouts' I thought, as I tramped past hedgerows which thinly screened scattered farmhouses beyond them. Another junction, another fingerpost. This one was called 'Beara', and had a wooden bench next to it, which I gratefully sat on to glug some water from my bottle. The temperature was checked. 22°. No wonder I felt hot and tired. But I must also have been slightly fitter as, although the hills were, shall we say, 'testing', I manged to conquer them one by one with, by now, minimum of rest stops. I looked at the fingerpost. South Molton – 4 miles.

The road between Kings Nympton and George Nympton I considered very beautiful. A downhill stretch with tall trees with overhanging branches protected us from the warm sunshine. Meadows on either side of us and dotted with sheep, disappeared from our view. No traffic passed us – all was quiet apart from birdsong, and the noise of the wind rustling the trees. It reminded me of the Dartmoor lanes.

Over another non-descript waterway and another hill to ascend. At the top was a house called 'Rosebud', where I stopped at the gate. Over a small hedge I could see some alpacas in a field. As I stood and watched them for a minute, a guy in his late fifties came strolling towards me from the house. Running slightly ahead of him was one of the biggest dogs I had ever seen.
'It's mainly wolf', the guy told me, after I had explained what I was doing leaning on his gate.
'Ah', I responded, as I kept a wary eye on the animal.
My knowledge of wolves depleted, I waved him, and the monstrous animal, goodbye.

More ascents and descents were undertaken until we crossed the River Mole, near the 'Wampford Woodland Retreat' which, I found out later, is a cabin with a hot-tub overlooking an ancient woodland.

Another ascent and we were in George Nympton, but the hill continued on for another half mile. At the top, our target of South Molton lay ahead of us, nestled in a valley.

After another half mile of moderate trudgery, we arrived at 'Limers Lane', with three-quarters of a mile to go. With renewed vigour, we progressed along George Nympton Road, and were soon in the outskirts of South Molton – soon after, we entered the town on a road I didn't know, but I found my bearings quickly enough once we passed the road to the South Molton Community College on the right, as the Lynton football team had played there occasionally. We headed further into town, passing shops, garages, and take-away emporiums, until we reached Broad Street. Crossing the road, it was then just a short distance before we turned into Duke Street, where we were staying for the night at a B & B: number five to be exact.

We were welcomed into a large house by the owner, and shown our room for the night, which was spacious. Dumping our gear, it was time to hit a pub, but not before we had asked whether or not we could bring a takeaway of some description back to the house. The owner was fully in accord with this and said he would provide appropriate crockery and cutlery if needed We left the house and made our way down the hill back onto Broad Street. Just across the road was the Town Arms Hotel, where we purchased our celebratory lager shandies, and made our way out to the rear of the pub in the late afternoon sun, to an area which gave a certain amount of pretence to being a beer garden. A few locals were already present there, but I found a table with two chairs, and rolled a cigarette while Lee looked online for the nearest Chinese restaurant, which was only round the corner. One telephone call later and an order made to be collected in fifteen minutes, it was time for a proper beer. I made my way back into the bar to grab two pints, while Lee went off to collect our food. More locals were in the bar; a dozen or so rough looking guys without a full set of teeth between them, but it was good to see some familiar beers available. I trotted back outside and sat back at my adopted table at exactly the same time as the proprietor turned out his two large dogs into the area in which I sat. Recalling my meeting with the huge dog/wolf I had met earlier that day, these two would have only compared with it if put together. However, they were big enough for me to keep a wary eye on as I supped my beer.

Lee arrived a short while afterwards, swallowed his beer in two gulps, and suggested we go back to the accommodation for a Chinese Takeaway feast, which I agreed to readily, as at that point one of the dogs had taken a considerable interest in my boots. We upped and left, only detouring into the local Spar shop to purchase four bottles of lager to go with our meal.

A quiet dining experience followed as we were the only guests. The owner had left out the promised plates and cutlery for us, which proved useful, although we did both manage to spill some of the sauces onto the pristine, white tablecloth. Full to the brim, half an hour later we made our way upstairs to our room, put the television on and watched it without seeing anything. A text message from a friend informed me that the Lynton Football team had won 6-1 earlier, but their performance wasn't great. But a win's a win of course. Mileage for the day was calculated at 15.9. Two more days and we would have made it. I was tired and my body ached. A very comfortable bed ensured, once again, that I slept soundly.

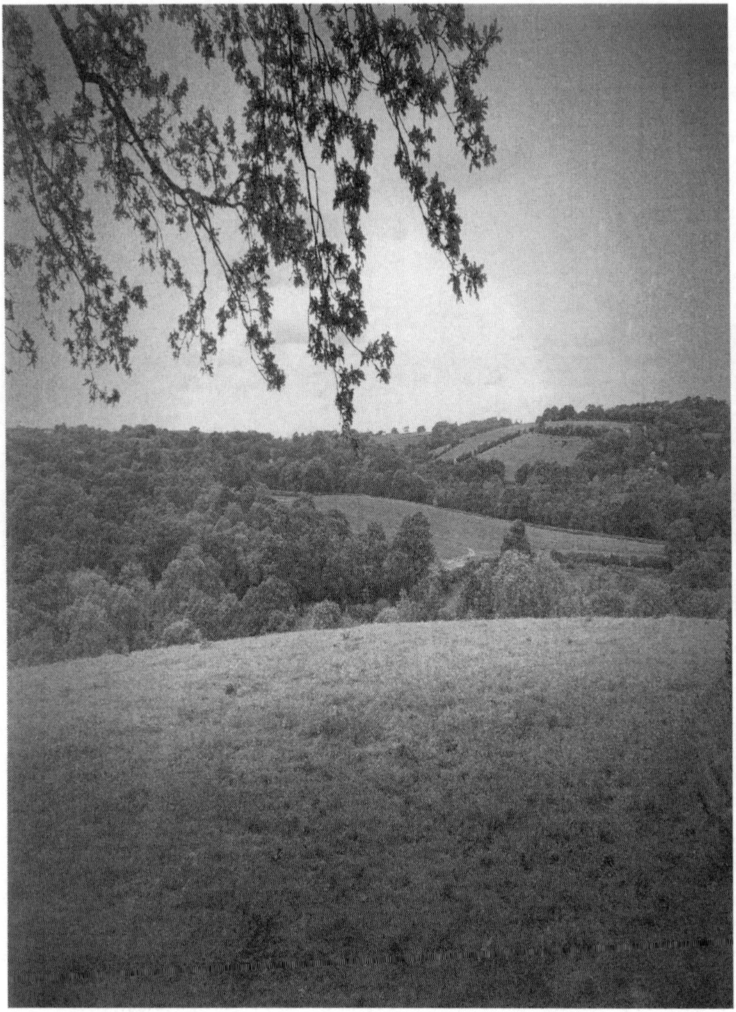

Thursday 25th

With a cappuccino in one hand and a cigarette in the other, I made my way downstairs and out of the front door into Duke Street. It was seven in the morning and the tall buildings shaded out any potential sunlight, making the road feel cool. The High Street looked busy enough at this hour, with traffic whizzing back and forth: Duke Street was devoid of any life apart from me and a black cat, which appeared out of an alleyway.

South Molton was originally called Dumnania, and was a robust town, mainly trading in wool up until the late 19th century. After this commodity moved up to North Yorkshire, the town's main role changed to tourism, being fed by a rail network on the Barnstaple to Taunton line, until Dr. Beeching wielded his axe in 1966 and closed it. Cars became more commonplace, and tourism continues to play an important part in its economy.

With nicotine and caffeine levels returned to normal, I wandered back to our room, made enough of a commotion so that Lee would stir from his slumber, ('Oh! Sorry! Did I wake you?' Followed by a silent 'heh heh') and jumped into the shower. Sluiced clean from my nights rest, Lee was unsurprisingly fully awake and sitting on the edge of his bed, staring at the map in our guidebook.

'I had a look at it last night,' I told Lee, 'and I had a thought.'

'So' he replied, 'anything new?'

'The way I see it,' I began, 'is that we're staying tonight in Withypool. Correct?'

'Correct.'

'If you look at the map, from Withypool to Lynmouth tomorrow we have to pass through Simonsbath.'

'Yep.'

'Well, as the distance from here to Withypool is just about the same as from here to Simonsbath, why don't we just walk to Simonsbath instead?'

Light dawned.

'Ah yeah', Lee agreed, 'we can get to the pub at Simonsbath, and get a taxi back to Withypool, stay overnight, and then taxi back to Simonsbath tomorrow morning.'

'Exactly. Just like we did at Lapford and back to Colebrooke. We're not cheating ourselves.'

'Sounds like a plan.'

I telephoned Kirsty and asked her to acquire us a taxi from the Exmoor Forest Inn that afternoon, going to Withypool.

'What time will you be there?' she asked.

'Ah.' I turned to Lee. 'What time do you think we'll get there?'

We consulted each other, as Kirsty was left hanging on to our conversation and becoming more impatient.
Consultation over. 'Let's go for five o'clock,' I told her.
'Ok, I'll sort it. Have a nice day.'
She's an angel.
We wandered downstairs for our obligatory fry up and devoured it readily.

So, we were going to go to Simonsbath, instead of Withypool. When I first arrived in the area more than ten years ago, I found out that Simonsbath was actually pronounced 'Simmonsbath' – a bit of a Devon thing, which made me laugh. Nowadays, being part of Devon myself, it 'makes I larf' instead. However one pronounces it, why Simonsbath is called Simonsbath appears to be a matter of conjecture. The 'bath' element is simple enough: apparently it is derived from the Old English 'baeth', which meant 'water', or 'pool'. The 'Simon' element however, is somewhat more of a problem – either it was just a common name, or, as legend has it, an individual called 'Simon', was a great hunter who had a stronghold at a place called Symonsburrow, supposedly an area in the Blackdown Hills. Who knows?

I rearranged my backpack, by now somewhat lighter with fewer clothes and the scant remainder of our flapjack supply. After thanking our host, I waited outside the house with our backpacks, while Lee disappeared to the Spar shop in the High Street to purchase more water. On his return, we shared out the water bottles – another two-litre bottle and two 500 ml bottles apiece. On went the backpacks and we headed up Duke Street to the Methodist Church at the top where we then headed down a gentle hill along North Street. We arrived in Station Road at the bottom which in turn, led us down to the main A361 road, which links Barnstaple to the M5, twenty-five miles away to the south. The junction of the A361 was adorned with roadworks and, although I tried to directly cross the road, I was accosted by an officious roadworker who informed me that I had to backtrack and use the underpass. Feeling grumpy at being told what to do, I sullenly retraced my steps fifty metres and walked down the footpath which led under the road to the north side of the A361. In front of us was a hill – nay, a daunting uphill terror, all the way into North Molton.

I knew the hill well, having driven up it many times. To ensure the survival of our feet and placate our heart rates, we decided to circumvent the main hill by turning right into a small road called Marsh Lane. We walked past the 'Riverside Caravan Park' and found ourselves heading onto a footpath which ran alongside the River Mole.

From here, the walk became very pleasant, and, as some sort of bonus, was well paved, with the inclusion of some duckboards which had been installed in the wettest areas. After a short while, we halted by a gate on which was an ominous sign: 'Beware of the Bull'. We looked at each nervously and discussed whether we should risk it, while a couple of damselflies, completely ignorant of our current dilemma, copulated on one of the duckboards a short distance away. We decided to chance it – there were plenty of trees in the meadow beyond; indeed, it looked more like an orchard, so there would be opportunity to evade an irate lumbering bovine should it appear. In the end, we crossed the picturesque meadow adjacent to the sunlit River Mole, with our sensory organs on full alert, and reached a farmgate at the other end with no incident at all. So the sign, warning us of deranged cattle, had been irrelevant.
'Maybe the sign should have read 'Beware of the Bullshit'', I remarked. Lee nodded. But for all we knew, there could have been a psychopathic bull hiding out of sight, sizing us up. We would never know. For the time being, we were intact, and still alive.

The footpath then became surrounded by woodland, became steep, then steeper and steeper, and urged us onwards and upwards to North Molton. We responded accordingly, with deep breathing and profuse sweating. As we ascended, we suddenly emerged from the trees and into bright, warm sunshine. Close to being out of breath, we eventually staggered off the footpath onto a small roadway called Dure Lane. The council workers responsible for naming and installing the road sign probably meant to name it 'Endure Lane', but, like our current situation, had probably run out of breath at the time and decided to shorten it. Two hundred yards later we stumbled into East Street, where I collapsed onto a metal bench situated directly across the road and alternated my cooling down by first pouring water over my head and then down my throat.

The hill hadn't finished with us yet. Another trek uphill for some four hundred yards was required, in conjunction with gritted teeth; I slouched up the hill, the only time I pretended I wasn't suffering was when I passed a scantily clad attractive woman, who was applying a coat of gloss to a front door. We trudged past one of the local pubs – The Miner's Arms: a hint of a past life. The Post Office and General Store (both of which were closed), were trudged past, and we eventually reached the square at the top by the All Saints Church, opposite The Poltimore Inn, named after Lord Poltimore, who, nearly two hundred years ago, owned most of the parish. After another rapid water glugging session, we headed off, uphill again, in the direction of Heasley Mill. Again, I knew the road well, having driven along it many times. At this hour it would be quiet enough: the only time I had known this particular stretch of road 'busy', was when I used to return from work and would get caught up in the school bus run – navigating a way past minibuses full of schoolkids in the narrow lanes became an artform.

We walked along the gently undulating back lane for nearly a mile, with large trees protecting us from the direct glare of the sun. At the junction of Bampfylde, we rested for a few minutes on a rickety wooden bench. Simonsbath was fingerposted three miles away. Our gaze flicked from the view across North Devon, which was pleasingly scenic, to my ordnance survey map.

'There's a footpath' commented Lee, 'which cuts the corner off.'

'Where?'

'Just here' said Lee, pointing at the map.

I took the map and screwed my eyes into focus. There was a footpath. It didn't look like it would save much but, a save is a save, after all. The map was folded away into a shape that bore a faint resemblance as to how it had emerged from its initial pristine folded shape, and we headed downhill toward Heasley Mill.

The lane was less busy than the one we had previously just walked, as if that was at all possible. The sun shone directly onto the road and a faint breeze moved the weakest tree branches high above our heads. Roughly two-thirds of the way down the hill, Lee espied the footpath sign.
'Here it is!' he exclaimed triumphantly.
I peered into the gloom beyond.
'That looks a bit overgrown' I remarked.
'It'll be fine' Lee responded, and dove into the darkness.
I followed suit – but not for long. Five yards to be exact. The footpath had obviously been little used and was heavily overgrown. In addition, underfoot was a mixture of slippery lumps of flint and shale, where a misplaced step could easily result in a broken ankle. Lee was doggedly determined to carry on, whereas I said I would go back to the road and walk down something a little more solid. As Lee disappeared further into the gloom, accompanied by the sounds of kicked flint and bramble tendrils scratching along clothing, I backtracked to the road, forcing my way through a stubborn hedge as I did so.

Removing a relatively reasonable amount of foliage from my person, I continued my journey alone down the hill, which became steeper every time one of my feet touched asphalt. I arrived in Heasley Mill and saw Lee chatting to a couple of residents – he appeared to be unscathed from his recent intrepid experience. I wandered up, exchanged pleasantries, gathered from the residents that the footpath hadn't been used properly for about twenty years, said farewell, and continued with our walk, past an old red telephone box. At the corner was a fingerpost which indicated Simonsbath to be six miles away. Hang on a minute! Before our descent into Heasley Mill, a fingerpost had indicated three miles. I looked at the map again. That couldn't be right. The route we were taking went almost straight to Simonsbath. And I couldn't believe it was six miles from here. So, either the mileage indicated on this post was wrong, or the post called 'Bampfylde' was. I don't know. Country folk with their country ways. I took a mouthful of water, shrugged, and commenced onto a moderate incline. We wandered past 'The Old Chapel', a place I had once considered purchasing, although almost all of the roof had caved in. What remained of the building – the four walls were in place at least – still retained an air of beauty.

We walked parallel to the River Mole along a quiet lane, bordered by earth banks and trees. It was all uphill, but the gradient was kind, so I didn't have to employ my targeted rest stop strategy. On reflection, either the gradient was kind, or my fitness had improved a little more. With Lee preceding me at his customary quarter-mile distance, I trudged along, alone again in my thoughts, as Lee probably did the same. The River Mole remained on my right, sometimes quite close to the road; the sunlight made it sparkle as it rushed past me in the opposite direction. I paused atop a small bridge under which a small tributary flowed. It really was incredibly beautiful and peaceful. I was slowly beginning to come around to the fact that although it was hard work, I was really pleased that I had made the decision to go on this journey. Progression had diminished the doubts.

The hill became steeper as we continued. We reached the Fyldon fingerpost and turned left toward Bentwitchen (three-quarters of a mile) and Simonsbath (five miles). There was a slight respite from hill-climbing to one of hill-descending, as we crossed a small stream at Lower Fyldon. Slight respite over, we then tackled Fyldon Hill which seemed, to me anyway, to be endless. In fact, Fyldon Hill is approximately two miles in length, with a gradient that exceeded not only my comfort zone, but also my perceived fitness increase. To be blunt, it was not far short of being murderous. Doubt reared its head again and began to surreptitiously interfere with my progress. But of course, at this stage of the endeavour, it was far beyond the point of giving up.

With the facial expression of a small boy being slobbered over by a large, elderly aunt, and, after numerous stops for leg-stretches, I finally made it to the top where Lee was waiting, looking slightly redder than normal. He confessed to me that the hill had, indeed, 'been a challenge'. It was time to have a rest. I sat down on an earth bank and surveyed the countryside around me. Behind me and still there, far off in the distance like a ghostly memory, were the shadows of Dartmoor. I couldn't believe it was still visible, but now, it was a long, long way behind me. That would be the last time I caught a glimpse of it on this journey.

I crossed the road junction and made my way to Kinsford Gate, hearing, and eventually seeing, the light traffic on the back lane which runs between Simonsbath and South Molton. A silent, sun-drenched walk (the temperature was 21° at this point) rewarded me with views of a Merlin hovering just over a field on my left, and a Bullfinch squatting on a fencepost. The silence was shattered soon after however, as a Wessex helicopter put in an appearance, flew above us, and then disappeared over a hill, only to reappear a minute or so later, repeating the performance for about fifteen minutes. I was unsure who they were and what they were doing: some form of training I supposed.

Lee was waiting at Kinsford Gate by a fingerpost which indicated Simonsbath three miles away. So, the post back at Bampfylde had been wrong after all. Damn those Bampfylde fingerpost constructors! Whoever they were. We walked up a smallish incline, then down Kinsford Hill, and over the small bridge at Kinsford Water. Another uphill section of around half a mile saw us rewarded with the county sign of Somerset.
'We're in Somerset?' spluttered Lee.
'Ooh arr', I replied in the best West Country accent I could muster. 'Devon's a bit of an odd-shaped county hereabouts' I explained to Lee, 'and we're on the eastern side of it.'

The road became slightly busier, but we managed to keep a look out for each other, shouting if a car was approaching. We generally walked facing the traffic, as per the Highway Code, unless there was right hand bend appearing, where we would walk along the left-hand side, so we could see any traffic, and any traffic could see us. We pushed on and reached the top of the hill: the resident fingerpost informed us that Simonsbath was one and a half miles away. We had a final rest by a farm gate before our descent to our finishing point. All the way down the hill were clear views of Exmoor, and it has always been one of my favourite views. I had always wanted to walk around this particular area, and now I was doing it. It really is an area of outstanding natural beauty, and I was seeing it dressed at its best.

It was a pleasure to finish our walking day downhill. We crossed the bridge over a sparkling River Barle: one of the sources we had left behind us as we walked down Kinsford Hill, the other was close to Exe Head, a place we would be visiting the next day. We walked past the sawmill, which is water-driven, and still uses machinery from the 19th century. The sawmill was bought in 1996 by the Exmoor National Park Authority, who intended using it to make gates and footpath signposts. Aha! The mystery of the erroneous Bampfylde fingerpost was potentially now solved. In 2010 production was stopped (probably because too many incorrect fingerposts were manufactured): the sawmill is now operated by volunteers.

From the sawmill, within a few minutes we stumbled into the beer garden of The Exmoor Forest Inn, at exactly four o'clock. We had enquired about a one night stay here, but the costs had seemed a little prohibitive at the time. For now, it was time to relax in the afternoon sunshine with our customary lager shandies, and chat about our day.

Where we sat was originally known as the Refreshment House. In 1885, the name was changed to The William Rufus Inn: less than twenty years later, the name changed again to The Exmoor Forest Hotel. It settled on its current name, reinstating the term 'Inn' whilst undergoing restoration in 2005.

When it was known as the William Rufus Inn, apparently it was the haunt of a renowned Exmoor Highwayman called Tom Faggus, a sort of a Robin Hood figure. At some point, Faggus married 'Girt Jan Ridds' sister, who you can read about in 'Lorna Doone'. All this sounds a bit dubious however, as the novel is set a century earlier, and the book itself was published in 1869 – fifteen years or so before The William Rufus Inn came to be.

A message from Kirsty earlier had informed me that the taxi would arrive at five-thirty, which it did. In the meantime, there was plenty of opportunity for another pint of proper ale. Charlie, a driver with Riverside Taxi Company who I see fairly regularly, materialised on time, wearing an incredulous look.

'What are you doing out here?' he asked. I explained our reason for being where we were, which he accepted with 'you must be nuts.' We threw our backpacks into the boot of his car, and undertook the fifteen-minute journey to Withypool, arriving outside The Royal Oak Inn just before six. With a promise from Charlie that someone would be with us tomorrow morning at half past nine, we entered the pub which was devoid of life. After a couple of minutes, we located someone who assisted us with our room, and also booked us a table for dinner.

Beds adorned with the contents of our backpacks, mileage calculated (11.5), showers undertaken, and a cup of coffee for good measure, we returned downstairs to the dining area which, by now, was fairly packed with customers. It was to be our last overnight stay of the trip so there was a feeling of 'let's splash out a bit and have something different.' I perused the menu intently for quite some time, while the waitress hovered impatiently.

'I'll have the pie and chips please,' I said.

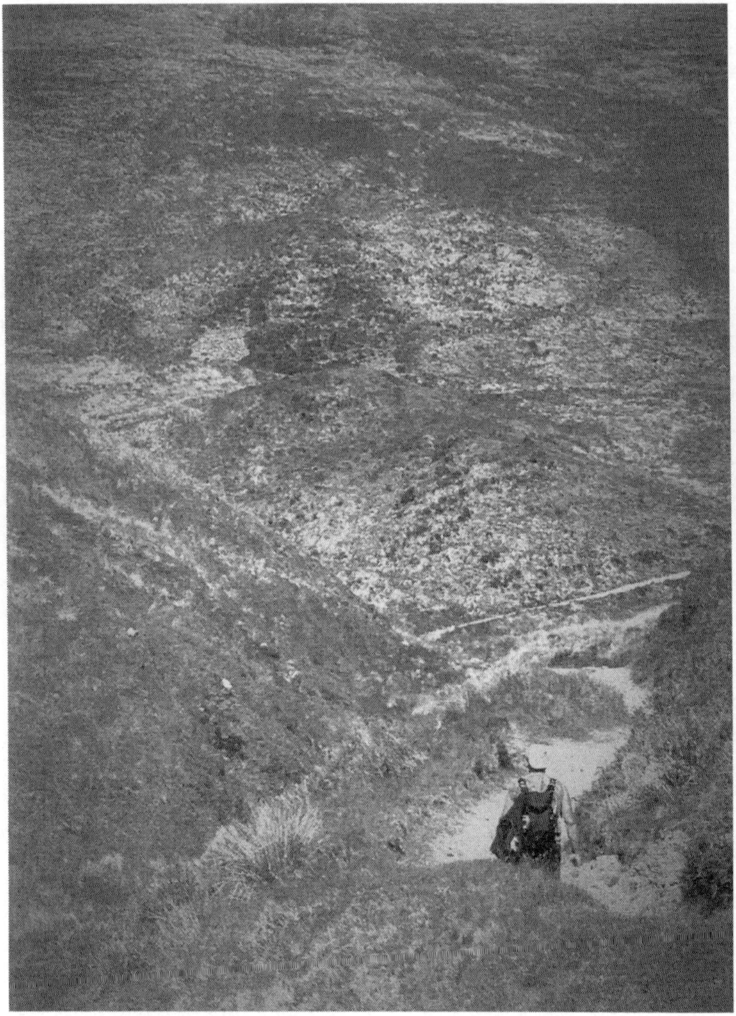

Friday 26th

I sat outside at the bottom of a metal staircase for my morning infusions. As it had been throughout our journey, the sun was already high up in its blue background. An elderly woman walked past me, adorned with a large backpack. I nodded at her as she passed me by, heading downhill to the river half a mile away. I returned to my morning thoughts. It was half past seven, and I was devoid of any. All was quiet – it felt more like a Sunday morning.

Withypool is pretty old - apparently inhabited since the bronze age. The elderly woman who I had nodded to, looked like she had been born around the same time. Withypool acquired its name from the willow trees adjacent to the river: the term 'withy' describing the willow stems used to weave baskets. The Royal Oak Inn, where I sat squinting at my coffee in the sunshine, was built in the 17th-century. A couple of celebrities have stayed at the inn, including RD Blackmore, who apparently wrote some of Lorna Doone in the bar. General Dwight D Eisenhower also propped up the bar a week before the planned D-Day landings in 1944. Overshadowing them both however, was the overnight stay undertaken by myself and Lee.

I wandered back up to our room, through a maze of small corridors, and immersed myself into the shower. At half past eight, Lee and I tucked into our final fry-up of the journey; an hour later Teresa from the Riverside Taxi Company stood in the doorway ready to collect us for our return journey to Simonsbath. Overnight, our water bottles had been refilled and placed in the fridge, so we had our supply for the day. We stepped out from the cab at The Exmoor Forest Inn and dumped our backpacks onto a grass verge where they could be sorted. Large boulders were put in use as something to sit upon as we undertook our backpack sorting duties.

Around ten o'clock, we headed off. The official Two Moors Way loops behind the pub and across some fields, before rejoining a road a mile up the hill. As the guide indicated that the fields were always wet and muddy, even during dry weather, Lee and I decided to walk along the road and pick up with the official route at the top of the hill. We walked back in the direction we had arrived from the day before, to the sawmill at the bottom of the hill, where the small bridge crosses over the River Barle. Lee complained jokingly that we should have been dropped at this point, as we had already walked this bit. Ignoring the turn off for Challacombe on our left, and gawping at the road sign which indicated that Lynton was nine miles away, we headed due north, uphill, on the B3223.

Almost at the top of the hill, the Two Moors Way rejoined us via a gate on our right. Two hundred yards further on, we left the road and became part of the Two Moors Way ourselves: a footpath at the back of a layby, with steps into a field, indicated the way we should go. We were, apparently, at a place called Prayway Head. The guidebook instructed us to pass through two gates, and then bear across an area called Dure Down, at a heading of 288°, towards Exe Head.

A herd of cattle were there to meet us as we passed through the second gate, but fortunately they were disinterested in us, and wandered off over a small rise to our right. We continued on our bearing and crossed a couple of other pathways just before Exe Head. According to our book, we were now at one of the remotest places on Exmoor. We passed through a gate and followed the directions on a signpost to Hoar Oak – a small river I knew well enough. Looking up, I knew exactly where I was, as I could see the Foreland Point lighthouse in the far distance ahead of me.

We then had the pleasure of walking through the Chains Valley, a truly beautiful place which I never knew existed. Having lived in Lynton for ten years, I chastised myself for not having been here before. I really should get out more. The rivers Exe, Barle and West Lyn all have their sources here, and the path we were on is also part of another walk, the Tarka Trail. Lee was excited to see a source of a river and photographed the area many times.

At a gate, we headed down to the bottom of the valley, crossed the Hoar Oak, and ascended the hill on the other side, arriving at a solitary tree – the Hoar Oak itself, which marked a boundary of a Royal Forest. Wandering up a track, we found ourselves, for the next two miles, walking along Cheriton Ridge, another place I never knew existed. Although I'm probably biased toward Exmoor and, having now completed my journey, I can honestly say that the last day, across Exmoor, was truly the most breathtaking and picturesque of it all. And all of it, is right on my doorstep. And no element of the bias was contributed to by the fact that I was nearly home. The Chains Valley and Cheriton Ridge are just simply stunning.

Halfway along the pleasant undulating Cheriton Ridge, heading to the hamlets of Cheriton and Scoresdown, we had to navigate our way past a herd of Exmoor ponies, which had a rather feisty small chaperone, who was obviously intent on guarding them from anything that moved. The obviously aroused male, who looked like he had five legs, we nicknamed 'Tony the Pony'. He bared his teeth at us as we gingerly passed the herd at a safe distance. As we did so, from the direction of Cheriton came two girls on cantering horses, accompanied by a dog, which put Tony on full alert. As they approached the herd, the dog decided to investigate the ponies which catapulted Tony into full angst. The girls desperately tried to call the dog back, but it was engaged in a full barking tease, which Tony was having none of and made it quite clear by whinnying and stamping his hooves. After a minute or so, the dog thought better of the situation and ran after the girls.

Once we were at, what we considered, to be a safe distance from Tony, we sat on some rocks in $20°$ heat and polished off our final flapjacks. We looked at the views around us as we downed some of our remaining water, and both agreed that the whole area was really very lovely. After fifteen minutes or so, we continued toward the farm buildings in the distance: two of the buildings I knew well enough, along with their owners, one of whom allows me to store bits of an old British Norton motorcycle in there, under the pretext that I am 'restoring it'. I will get around to it.

The Two Moors Way veers away to the right, into Cheriton, which is the way Lee headed. I decided to go straight to the farm buildings and through the yard, which is what a lot of Two Moors Way walkers do unknowingly. As I entered the yard, I thought about knocking on the owner's door, or the neighbours, and requesting a cup of tea. But I didn't. I'd already walked through their field and yard without asking - they may have been watching me from their windows. I waited in the lane in Scoresdown for a few minutes before Lee appeared from my right, having walked into Cheriton: a few minutes down the road from where I stood.

Back together, we walked down Cheriton Road, which, as far as vehicles are concerned, is impassable. A steep downhill lane, riddled with potholes, precludes even the most hardiest of local tractor drivers, who all give it a wide berth. At the bottom of the hill, we crossed a bridge over Hoar Oak Water, next to a house called Lower Scoresdown. I love the house, and at one point had viewed it when it came up for sale a few years back. But the timing wasn't right and sadly someone else, for whom the timing was right, bought it and has been there ever since. After crossing the bridge, we went through a gateway on our right and entered Combe Park.

Sitting on a bench were a couple who we had bumped into previously on our journey. I told them that we were nearly there, and if they wanted life to be easy, not to follow the Two Moors Way at the Hillsford Bridge junction, but merely cross the road and follow the river all the way down to Lynmouth. But as they had undertaken the Two Moors Way in its entirety, I think they had resigned themselves to the fact that they were going to complete it all. Lee and I took off through Combe Park – an area in which I had exercised the dogs regularly when they were younger.

We passed the Combe Park Hotel, a luxurious looking sprawl, which functions primarily as a provider for weddings and business meetings, and made our way to the carpark, where a nearby Edwardian building called Combe Park Lodge is situated. Just beyond the Lodge, the end of the park terminates at a junction of the main A39 road at Hillsford Bridge. At this point, the official route continues straight ahead, upwards, passing an Iron Age settlement, towards an area called 'The Cleaves'. There, the path descends steeply into a gorge and then ascends back out of it. The subsequent final descent into Lynmouth is almost vertical. I felt like I had undertaken more than my fair share of ups and downs, so Lee and I crossed the river bridge and entered a gate on our left into the Watersmeet Estate.

Now it was just about downhill all the way. The walk to Watersmeet from Hillsford Bridge is only about half a mile, and there were a few walkers either heading to Watersmeet from Combe Park carpark, for a cream tea, or returning to Combe Park after having just had one. The house at Watersmeet dates from around 1832 and was built for an individual called Walter Stevenson Halliday. Originally a fishing lodge (there were many salmon in the river at that time) and a romantic retreat (it's presumed that there were a lot of romances going on as well), it has been a tea-room since 1901. Eventually acquired by the National Trust, they have continued dispensing tea, which accompany plain scones adorned in the correct manner with first, cream, then jam, in addition to being an information centre and a shop.

We didn't stop at Watersmeet, although it is an idyllic suntrap of a tea garden to sit in. Leaving crumbs on your table ensures visits from the many finches which inhabit the area. In the summer, there are also many colourful butterflies, and the lower river levels during the warmer months ensure that people can embrace the shallow parts of the river for a paddle, albeit at around

8°C. When friends of mine came to stay and their children wanted to play in the river, I told them it was 'solar-heated'.

With Watersmeet behind us, we passed by a bridge which Kirsty and I, having undertaken a walk to Watersmeet on a previous occasion, had nicknamed 'Chewing Gum Bridge', on account of us throwing small pieces of chewing gum into the river from it, and watching the small brown trout dart out of the margins to feast upon them. Up a small rise and down the other side, we then passed the remains of the 'Lynrock Mineral Water Company', which bottled water, as well as making ginger beer, up until 1939. The site was destroyed in the 1952 flood.

We crossed the river and followed the path down to Lynmouth. As we were nearly there, my pace inevitably quickened; my gait was similar to a new-born lamb on steroids. Lee called from behind me, 'take it steady'; I responded with 'shut up.' On the outskirts of Lynmouth, I telephoned Kirsty, who was waiting outside The Rising Sun, a pub right next to Lynmouth Harbour, to let her know that my calculations were wrong, and we would be another hour at least.
'Really?' she asked.
'No' I owned up, 'not really. We'll be with you within ten minutes.'

We arrived in Lynmouth at just about three o'clock, and Kirsty was waiting outside the pub with two bottles of ice-cold Exmoor Gold Ale, my favourite local beer. Kirsty's godmother, Sally, said I looked like a refugee from the Minehead Butlin's camp. Kirsty didn't immediately recognise me at first, as I was dressed in my baseball cap which I had continued to wear back to front, a ragged, sweaty tee shirt, and a pair of shorts. My backpack still had my waterproof jacket hanging off it. My appearance, courtesy of the sun, covered just about all of the spectrum between red and brown. In all honesty, I looked like a dustbin on legs.

We wandered around the corner to 'The Walker' statue, shook hands with it, and stood there, posing for photographs. With the ale half swallowed, Lee and I wandered across the road and into the Lynmouth National Park Centre, or the Exmoor Centre Pavilion as we know it, and signed the book. I didn't feel in anyway like I had cheated. We had set out with a clear intention of walking across Devon – if that included taking in some of the Two Moors Way along the way, then so be it. We totalled our mileage – 98.6. Should we walk another 1.4, just to round it up? Not a chance.

As Lee leant on a wall and gazed at the Bristol Channel, I went onto Lynmouth Beach and collected two, small, black pebbles – one for him, and one for me.

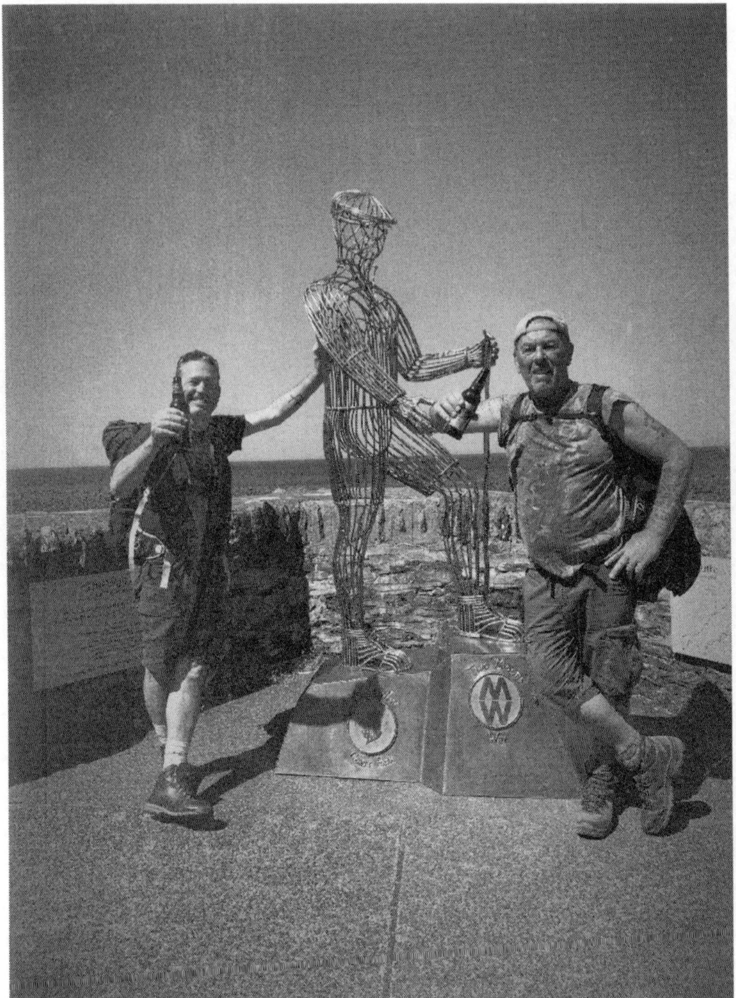

Postscript

The walk had been successfully completed. We had walked across Devon, from coast to coast, and intermittently walked along bits of the Two Moors Way. My weight had dropped by half a stone, and local walks during the subsequent summer I found easier.

The party was held the day after our completion and was attended by around one hundred and fifty people. To be fair, most of them were probably there to see the band, rather than celebrate my triple milestone. But that didn't matter. It was a great day.

About a month later, I caught up with Lee via a telephone conversation. Strangely, we both felt that we missed the walk we had just undertaken, and we really should put something together for 2024. But where? I looked at 'The Great Glen Walk', along the shores of Loch Ness. But as Lee pointed out, we might not be so lucky with the weather, so that idea was put on the backburner. Similarly postponed was a suggested walk through The Cairngorms. Insanely, I had purchased a copy of the Cicerone guide to walking the South-West Coast Path – a total of 630 miles. If we stuck to our overnight accommodation plan for that walk as we had with our coast to coast, the Coast Path would end up being a very expensive walk indeed.

In the end, we decided that during late April in 2024, we would undertake the Two Moors Way properly. So if you find that you have purchased this book from a shop somewhere either in Lynton or Lynmouth around this time, I'll probably be on the trail again as you read it.

I was chatting to someone in Lynmouth during the summer of 2023 about the walk. We were both leaning against the harbour wall, each of us with a pint in hand. As people do, we chatted about everything – most of it irrelevant. At one point he looked at me quizzically.

'Why did you do it?' he asked.

'What?'

'Your walk. Why did you do it?'

I had a well-rehearsed answer.

'It's simple,' I explained, 'one day I won't be able to.'

Printed in Poland
by Amazon Fulfillment
Poland Sp. z o.o., Wrocław